Lillian Too
Jennifer Too

FORTUNE & FENG SHUI

RABBIT

2021

KONSEPBOOKS
ASTROLOGY . FENG SHUI . INSPIRATIONS

Fortune & Feng Shui 2021 Rabbit

by *Lillian Too* and *Jennifer Too*
© 2021 Konsep Lagenda Sdn Bhd

Text © 2021 Lillian Too and Jennifer Too
Photographs and illustrations © Konsep Lagenda Sdn Bhd
Cover Art © Josh Yeo Zhu Lin

The moral right of the authors to be identified as authors of this book has
been asserted.

Published by KONSEP LAGENDA SDN BHD (223 855)
Kuala Lumpur 59100 Malaysia

For more Konsep books, go to *www.lillian-too.com* or *www.wofs.com*
To report errors, please send a note to errors@konsepbooks.com
For general feedback, email feedback@konsepbooks.com

ISBN 978-967-329-296-7
Published in Malaysia, September 2020

RABBIT 2021

BIRTH YEAR	WESTERN CALENDAR DATES	AGE	KUA NUMBER MALES	KUA NUMBER FEMALES
Fire Rabbit	2 Feb 1927 - 22 Jan 1928	94	1 East Group	5/8 West Group
Earth Rabbit	19 Feb 1939 - 7 Feb 1940	82	7 West Group	8 West Group
Metal Rabbit	6 Feb 1951 - 26 Jan 1952	70	4 East Group	2 West Group
Water Rabbit	25 Jan 1963 - 12 Feb 1964	58	1 East Group	5/8 West Group
Wood Rabbit	11 Feb 1975 - 30 Jan 1976	46	7 West Group	8 West Group
Fire Rabbit	29 Jan 1987 - 16 Feb 1988	34	4 East Group	2 West Group
Earth Rabbit	16 Feb 1999 - 4 Feb 2000	22	1 East Group	5/8 West Group
Metal Rabbit	3 Feb 2011 - 22 Jan 2012	10	7 West Group	8 West Group

Cover Art by Josh Yeo Zhu Lin

Features an agile Rabbit under a bright sky with both sun and moon. In 2021, the Rabbit enjoys the Peach Blossom Star, bringing romance and enhanced relationship luck.

CONTENTS

Chapter Three

Chapter Four

CONTENTS

Introduction to the Year 2021

Chapter 1

YEAR OF THE METAL OX

The coming year is the Year of the Metal Ox, a year when harvests are reaped as a result of old-fashioned hard work. It takes on the nature of the diligent Ox, whose finest qualities are its stability and steadfastness, the sign that symbolizes all the hard work that has to be done in order to prepare for the harvests and prosperity that follows. While the coming year can be prolific, there are few shortcuts to be had. Those who put in the hours and who match their effort with their wit will be those who reap the most from the year. This will not be a time for easy money or overnight speculative gains. It will be a year when substance wins out over panache, and when those who put emphasis on building solid foundations will prosper. One should strive to work first at what one can bring to the table, before making promises or trying to convince others of one's potential.

THE TOILING OX

This is the year of the Metal Ox, so it is one in which the Earth element of the Ox gets constantly exhausted by its heavenly stem of Metal. Earth produces Metal, so is exhausted by it. This is a year when the Ox has to constantly keep up its efforts to stay ahead. Individuals who are dedicated and disciplined will be the most effective and the most successful.

The year can be an industrious one, but only if one acts industriously. There is good progress to be made for those who consciously and actively mirror the attributes of the steady Ox. It will be a year void of lightning speed success but conscientious work pays off. It is a year that rewards hard work over talent, where practice trumps winging it.

FORMIDABLE FRIENDS AND FOES

The Ox sign makes a loyal friend but also a formidable enemy, so the year will see both sides of this coin. Competitive pressures will be tough, but those with robust teams of collaborators and allies will succeed. Factions will form and there will be both poignant friendships and daunting foes. Those that stand alone will find it difficult to navigate through the various obstacles that the year offers up.

The Paht Chee of 2021 features both a troublesome clash and a promising alliance in its earthly branch line up. There is a clash between the Ox and the Sheep in the Day Pillar, but also an encouraging connection between the Ox and the Rat in the Hour Pillar. It is a year when friendships matter, so one must work at keeping one's friends. Those that slip the net to the other side could become intimidating enemies. People will tend to hold grudges and have long memories. The advice is to avoid offending the wrong people with careless words and unthinking actions. Skins

are thin and offense is taken at the smallest acts of
offhandedness.

THE LEADER REIGNS SUPREME

The twelve months from February 4th 2021 to February
4th 2022 will support people in leadership positions.
Those who have recently risen to high office or who
were promoted last year, whether in Government or in
Commerce, will feel the benefits of the year's energies.
Such individuals enjoy the buoyancy of the winds and
waters that translate into a powerful flow of auspicious

PAHT CHEE CHART 2021			
HOUR	DAY	MONTH	YEAR
壬	癸	庚	辛
Yang Water	Yin Water	Yang Metal	Yin Metal
壬 子	己 未	甲 寅	己 丑
Yang Water Rat	Yin Earth Sheep	Yang Wood Tiger	Yin Earth Ox

heaven luck. They benefit from a special vitality that aids their decision-making. Their actions carry weight and they find it easy to garner support for what they want to do.

With the #6 Heaven Star taking center stage in the year's Flying Star chart, leaders and those in positions of power are blessed with the mantle of heaven. It instills in them great authority and effect over their charges so they will have greater ability to influence the outcome of what they are engaged in.

This year favours leaders, chiefs, bosses, managers and directors of all kinds, and in all fields.

The danger this year is that the #7 afflictive star has arrived in the NW, the sector that represents the Patriarch. With leaders so powerful and with the treacherous #7 star in its home location, this brings the risk that those in power may use their position for harm rather than for good. Leaders with strong moral ethics can effect very positive change with a big and lasting impact, but those who act on a whim could end up making disastrous decisions that affect the fortunes of many.

The presence of the Ox-Sheep clash in the chart suggests that while leaders may be powerful within their own spheres, they meet with hostility from opposing interest groups, and leaders of other nations and organizations. Different blocs will have differing agendas, and when compromises cannot be reached, there will be conflict and struggle.

On the world stage, the influence of the #7 on the leader suggests there will be much fighting energy, and even risk of war. US-China trade relations will continue to deteriorate, with effects impacting more and more nations. Worrying alliances may be formed. There will be unified groups but it will not be one unified assembly; there will be powerful diverse groups that clash and clatter.

Conspiracy theorists may well have some premise to their conjectures; this becomes ever more likely if the ominous influence of the excessive Metal in the year's chart is not strongly suppressed. All may not be what it seems to be on the surface

THE INFLUENCE OF THE ELEMENTS

METAL *represents authority*

METAL in 2021 stands for RESOURCES, but it also stands for AUTHORITY. Unfortunately, in 2021, authority may not always be benevolent. This year there is almost too much Metal energy, and too much makes the ominous side of this element stronger. Leaders become more powerful, and power here has to potential to corrupt. Checks and balances become more important, as the year could produce leaders who make unscrupulous decisions, taking into account only their own personal agendas.

This affliction affects not just leaders on the world stage but those in one's immediate sphere as well – bosses, community leaders, mentors, teachers, parents. If this Metal energy is not kept under control, it could lead to disastrous consequences in one's personal daily life. The effects of this can feel very real and close to home.

WHAT TO DO: We suggest displaying a **red-faced Kuan Kung,** the powerful Warrior God in the home and office to protect against the excess of Metal element energy. Having this God of War and God of Wealth in the home ensures you stay on the winning side of the element luck effect. Kuan Kung will ensure you make judicious decisions that end up benefiting you and your family in the long run. Gives you courage to move forward but tempers any misplaced bravado.

Red-faced Kuan Kung
with 5 victory flags

2. Wearing jewellery in precious Metals fashioned as sacred syllables and symbols transforms the effect of Metal from autocratic to benevolent. It helps keep you protected from harm and ensures you do not lose the support of the people who matter most to your prospects in life- eg. Your boss, your parents, your teachers.

WATER *represents competition*

WATER in 2021 stands for FRIENDS and FOES, which are present in equal measure. Both have an equivalent part to play in the outcomes that follow. Because the year is one of STRONG WATER, the element of Water this year needs to be treated with caution. Too much of it could tip the scales over, attracting fierce rivalry and underhand tactics by one's competition, rather than cultivating strong allies that stay loyal.

This year it becomes especially important to carry protective amulets that guard against betrayal and disloyalty. Carrying an image of **Kuan Kung with Anti-Betrayal Amulet** will help protect against becoming a victim of these energies. Always give others suitable respect, and don't disregard the dangers of allies changing sides. If the incentive becomes attractive enough, they will. Don't take anything too personally if you can adopt the stoic outlook of the Ox where you make the most of the opportunities open to you without complaining too much what is fair or not fair. You can effectively buffer against many of the pitfalls of the year.

THE COLOR BLUE – Blacks and blues stand for Water energy. While water to the Chinese traditionally represents money, this year it also signifies competition. Using too much of this color this year holds the danger of fueling rivalry and competitiveness amongst one's peers. Do not don too much black, and when you do, try to add a splash of color to neutralize its more sinister effects. Place the **Celestial Water Dragon** in the home to keep this element under control.

FIRE *brings wealth*

FIRE in 2021 stands for WEALTH LUCK. This is the element that appears to be completely missing from the year's chart and thus is the one we must actively work at replacing. There is hidden wealth brought by the Tiger, but this needs a trigger for it to be actualized. We suggest wearing the color red in free abandon this year. Remember, this is the Year of the Ox, an Earth sign whose inner vitality gets spurred on by the wonderful energy of Fire.

THE COLOR RED - Red to the Chinese is always considered lucky. It is a color of celebration and carnival. It is traditionally used in all auspicious occasions, and as we move into the new year of 2021, it is especially important to wear plenty of red! For the first 15 days of the Lunar New Year, we recommend getting yourself a red outfit for each day. Keep up this ritual through the entire 15 days of celebrations to ensure its effects can get you through the year. This is an excellent way to "fuel up" for the year, as it is a year when the element of Fire is glaringly missing.

 In the home, keep the lights bright throughout the year. Change your lightbulbs whenever they start to flicker or lose energy, and don't try to save on the electricity bill by constantly turning off the lights! It is far more important to work at keeping this element properly energized through the year. Don't be penny wise and pound foolish. Lights represent Fire energy, and Fire energy represents wealth and prosperity in 2021.

NEW WEALTH WALLET: Each year it is an extremely lucky ritual to get yourself a new wallet and transfer some money from your old wallet over to your new one, while adding in some brand new notes (best if from cash received as a Chinese New Year ang pow, or from one's latest drawn salary or bonus). You can also keep an image of the **Wealth God Sitting on**

a Tiger in the form of a gold card inside your wallet; very auspicious as the Tiger is the sign that brings hidden wealth to the year.

Each year we design a wallet to vibrate and sync with the energies of the year, and for 2021, our wealth wallet features the stock market bull. It is the Year of the Ox and the Wall Street Bull is a most auspicious

symbolic cousin of the sign of the year. The Wall Street Bull represents your investments going up, and your asset wealth growing.

We also have the **Asset Wealth Bull** with Wealth Amulet which will attract wealth-generating luck to any home which invites it in. Display prominently in the West where the *Star of Current Prosperity* has flown to this year or on your desk in front of you where you work. The idea is to see it daily and its subliminal effects will magically influence your actions and ability to attract wealth luck into your life.

WOOD *brings growth*

WOOD is the element that stands for growth. In 2021, it also signifies intelligence and creativity. It is what brings fresh new ideas to the mix, encouraging a blossoming of imagination and ingenuity. As we foray further into the new decade, old ideas will increasingly lose appeal and old technologies become obsolete with increasing speed. These need to be replaced and they will, and it will be those who can dream up the new ideas, methods, designs and technologies that will profit.

For the individual looking at making it in a rapidly changing world, it will be enhanced creativity and thinking outside the box that will help you. Surround yourself with the vibrant energy of plants and greenery, invite fresh flowers displayed in auspicious vases into your living space. If you live in a modern skyscraper city where feasting on green is difficult or unusual, look for ways to introduce indoor gardens into your home and office space, take regular time to visit parks and gardens, or make time to visit the countryside to refuel and recharge your senses with the power of nature.

THE COLOR GREEN – Greens of all kinds represent innovation and vision in 2021. Fill your wardrobe with lots of this color in emerald green, lime green, neon green, shamrock, chartreuse, sage, seafoam… all of these will inject your wardrobe with a fresh dash of inspiration and will attract wonderfully inspired energies into your aura. Green this year is very lucky and brings to the wearer a new lease of life. If you have been feeling dull, uninspired or at a crossroads, introducing a pop of bright green into what you wear or carry will give you the boost you need to change track, get moving, get started. It is the "energizing" colour of the year and should be made use of liberally and profusely.

TEND TO YOUR GARDEN: There's nothing that invokes better yang Wood energy than thriving plants and greenery. Make a trip to your local nursery and bring home some vibrant new plants to add to your garden. If you live in an apartment, introduce some live potted plants into your living space. This will stir up the creative juices in you needed to dream up new ideas and to hatch ingenious strategies for your work and in your life.

EARTH *brings power & influence*
EARTH in the Year of the Ox is the intrinsic element of the animal sign of the year. It is the element that symbolizes stability, strength and permanence. It is the element that ensures that however crazy the energy gets,

however quickly the world changes around us, we can dig our heels deep and stay grounded with our values and our visions intact. Earth energy will prevent us being light-eared and light-headed, or easily influenced. In 2021, the element of EARTH also signifies recognition and power. It brings the luck of rank and position, and boosts one's chances when it comes to promotion and upward mobility, whether in one's career or in any climb to the top of any organization. Earth energy brings you influence and command and will make people listen to you.

EARTH COLORS – Wearing shades of earth tones brings you respect and makes people listen to you. It keeps you rational and well-balanced and envelops you with an aura of dependability. An excellent color group to use when you need others to take you seriously. Earth colors include yellow, orange, beige and cream, in all their shades. Wear such colors when you feel you need others to take notice of you, when you want to boost your influence over others and when you need people to listen to you. Those of you ambitious for your career to get a boost will benefit greatly from making use of earth colors.

THE 24 MOUNTAINS CHART OF 2021

The compass wheel around which the animals are positioned contain 24 mountains, which attract different stars each year. The overall fortunes of the year get enhanced or disabled depending on which

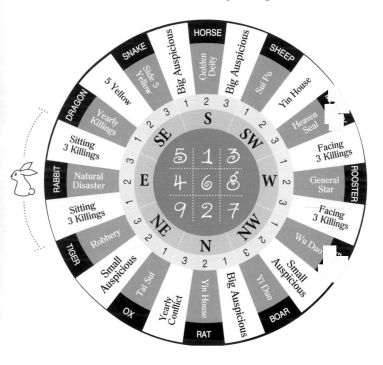

stars settle into which corners. Some years will have more auspicious stars, and some less, and their positions around the wheel impact on each animal sign differently.

THE LUCK OF BIG & SMALL AUSPICIOUS

One of the luckiest indications from this chart are the Big and Small Auspicious Stars, and in 2021, we have 5 of such stars making an appearance. The year enjoys three **Big Auspicious** stars and two **Small Auspicious** stars. The animal signs that benefit from these are the **Horse, Snake, Sheep, Rat, Boar**, the **Dog, Ox** and **Tiger**. The locations of these stars are spread out giving the above animal signs the potential to seize opportunities that come their way.

The sign that benefits most from this indication is the **HORSE**. The Horse enjoys two Big Auspicious stars, which suggests that after two difficult years, this sign is ready to take flight. The free-spirited Horse person can finally seize what it has been grappling after; this is a year when this sign can take risks and put wholehearted effort behind their passions. It is a year when the Horse should not rest on its laurels, because the big time has arrived.

The other signs enjoying Big Auspicious are the **Snake** and **Sheep**, and the **Rat** and **Boar**. These signs also have the potential to go after big dreams and, to

realize big ambitions they may have been harboring. For these signs, opportunities will be plentiful. Success comes for those who are hungry and resolute. Remember that this year, results do not come immediately, so one must not get discouraged if the path to actualization seems long or even impossible. The winners will be those with the staying power to keep at it and stay the course. Hold on to your dreams, and don't change your mind at every setback. Trust in your instincts and passions, and don't give power to those who disturb your mind or pour cold water on your ideas.

While the Stars of Big Auspicious bring really fabulous blessings, so do the Stars of Small Auspicious. These have the same effect as their big brother stars, but they bring success in smaller measures and in stages. The signs enjoying Small Auspicious this year are the **Ox**, **Tiger**, **Dog** and **Boar.** For these signs, they are likely

to meet with small successes that form the stepping stones to bigger success later on. For these signs, this is a year for building firm foundations and laying out the pathway for future triumphs.

Small Auspicious brings end goals that hold slightly longer time trajectories, but accompanied with the same staying power, success does ultimately come. Learn to celebrate the smallet of wins and stay clearheaded about your ultimate goals. If you constantly step back to examine the bigger picture, you will not lose sight of why you are doing what you're doing.

ENHANCER: Remember that *Stars of Big and Small Auspicious* bring the potential of great fortune, but to enjoy their benefits to the fullest, they need to be enhanced. Each year then, we design a Big Auspicious Enhancer to kickstart the very positive effects of these stars. This year, all animal signs benefit from displaying the **Six Birds Auspicious Multiplier**. This activator featuring an I-Ching coin with six birds and the auspicious amulet enhancer brings new opportunities. The 6 birds activates the #6 Heaven Star that rules the year's Lo Shu chart. The number 6 is the number of the heavens, which unlocks the celestial hand of the Gods. Display this potent activator in a place where you can see it often – either in a prominent place in the home, or in front of you on your work desk.

6 Birds Auspicious Multiplier. Unlocks the Big Auspicious luck of the year.

LUCK FROM THE HEAVENS

Two stars that further magnify the luck of the heavens are the *Golden Deity Star* and the *Star of the Heavenly Seal*. These land in the location of the **Horse** and the **Monkey**, bringing these two signs the luck of celestial fortunes. For these two signs, help comes without having to seek it. They enjoy the patronage of powerful mentors with many wishing to help them. They also have better instincts and can trust their own judgment more. For the Horse, as it also enjoys two Big Auspicious stars, little can go wrong as long as it stays judicious and diligent. The Monkey however needs to employ its trademark cunning to make the most of the Heaven Seal; it has to dodge the Yin House and Facing 3 Killings, but its main 24 Mountain star influence is extremely positive.

To make the most of these stars, we recommend that the Horse and Monkey invite in a **Golden Deity** into the home. Any Buddha, God or holy figure in line with your own faith will work. We particularly love **Kuan Yin, the Goddess of Mercy**, revered by Chinese all around the world. She is the female personification of the compassionate Buddha and brings wealth, health and happiness and protection from harm.

Kuan Yin

THE GENERAL STAR

The **Rooster** enjoys the *General Star*, which brings it power and authority, but unfortunately also fuels its short fuse and hot temper. But the Rooster this year has the very lucky #8 star, which enhances its fortunes and intrinsic energy. The Rooster as a sign does not suffer fool's gladly, so all these indications point to a Rooster that reigns supreme in 2021, but one who may be insufferable to those it considers "beneath" them, whether in intelligence or in status. To make the most of this star, all Roosters this year benefit from displaying the **Power Ru Yi**, the scepter of authority which boosts its command as boss or leader, while ensuring no disgruntled subordinates try to make trouble, or rivals rise up to try to displace it.

Star of the Yin House

This star brings danger of sickness and disease, and a general lack of energy to those it afflicts. It is particularly dangerous if one is already ill or elderly, or with other heavy afflictions indicated in their charts. This year, there are two Yin House stars and these arrive in the SW and North, affecting the **Sheep**, **Monkey** and **Rat**. All three of these signs are advised to take more care this year when it comes to health, well-being and safety. We strongly suggest that these signs carry protective amulets to shield them from the influence of malevolent spirits that may wreak havoc in their lives. Any of the **seed syllables Om, Ah or**

Hum will invoke the presence of the mighty Buddha, establishing a firm spiritual circumference of protection around the wearer.

If ill health is of particular concern, we recommend wearing and displaying health amulets. The **Wu Lou**, **Garuda Bird**, and the **Healing Deer**, bring precious cosmic protection. The deer is especially wonderful; this animal has always been associated with health, strength and vigor. It is also the animal that holds the solution to good health when all other methods have not seemed to work. There are many folk legends associated with the deer in all cultures, but in Chinese mythology, the deer is almost always shown accompanying Sau, the divine God of Longevity.

Healing Deer

The Robbery Star

This star brings money loss and betrayal and especially affects the **Tiger** in 2021. Those born under this sign need to be especially mindful not to get taken in by con men and getting cheated by others. There is higher chance of getting conned into undertaking bad investments. Business partners and associates could prove untrustworthy. It is also very important whenever one has this affliction to take care of personal safety. Robberies, muggings, petty thieves and street crime become more of a danger. This star also brings risk of becoming a victim of chance or collateral damage in somebody else's fight.

To counter this negative star, you need the image of the **Blue Rhino and Elephant** in the home, and you MUST carry the **Anti Robbery Amulet**. This protects against losing money and possessions. It is also important to protect against personal harm and injury; wear protective amulet at all times! Females in particular should avoid venturing out alone late at night or putting themselves under unnecessary risk; they should carry the **Nightspot Protection Amulet** for protection against petty crime.

Yearly Conflict & Yearly Killings

These stars bring obstacles to everything you do, making it difficult to make meaningful progress. These are the stars that can discourage you from remaining steadfast and keeping on your intended path. It throws up unexpected snags and hitches, and when left unchecked, can overwhelm one with feelings of depression and anxiety. These are negative stars that gather the slings and arrows of misfortune hurling them your way with some measure of ferocity. It is as such extremely important to take note of their location each year and take definite steps to neutralize them.

In 2021, the Yearly Killings star has landed in the **Dragon**'s location of SE1, and the Yearly Conflict Star visits the N3 sector, affecting the animal signs of **Rat** and **Ox**.

The *Yearly Killings Star* is deadlier and needs immediate action – we suggest that all Dragon-born and all those whose bedrooms or main door location are in the SE carry the **28 Hums Protection Wheel** and invite in the **Buddha image of Nangsi Zilnon Guru Rinpoche**. He is the warrior Buddha who completely overcomes all types of obstacles brought by the Yearly Killings.

28 Hums
Protection
Wheel

The *Yearly Conflict Star* makes everyone want to fight with you, bringing opposition to your ideas and making it difficult to see your projects through. Working in teams becomes especially difficult. At work, this could mean difficult colleagues and fierce politicking by workplace rivals. Those afflicted by this star could find themselves spending the better part of their time dodging potshots rather than focusing on their work. It makes work life very unpleasant, and the effects of this star can also permeate one's social and private life. This negative star arrives in the N3 sector affecting all whose main door or bedroom or office are located in this part of the home or office, and it affects Rat and Ox born people. Those affected by this affliction need to carry protection amulets and display the relevant cures. The **Dorje Drolo Scorpion Amulet** is especially helpful in this regard.

Natural Disaster Star

This star arrives in the East sector, affecting those who spend much time in this part of the home, and affecting all **Rabbit-born.** This is the star that puts in you in harm's way – being at the wrong place at the wrong time. It brings all manner of natural misfortune including floods, fires, earthquakes, tsunamis, viruses and disease. If you are afflicted by this star, you MUST carry spiritual protection. ALL East-facing homes benefit from inviting in a statue of **Guru Rinpoche**, and all Rabbit-born should wear the **Bhrum Pendant** which protects against all kinds of harm, illness, accidents and avoidable misfortune.

LUCK OF THE 12 ANIMAL SIGNS

Every animal sign is affected by a host of factors which change each year, producing a different basket of combinations which influence each individual sign's luck differently. Aside from the animal sign year you were born under, there are additional factors affecting your luck, but viewed together with these indications, anyone can alter the course of their lives and make intelligent decisions to maximize luck through any given year.

Here we summarize the broad outlook for the different animal signs, and in later chapters of this book, we go into greater depth and detail on what all of this means for you personally, depending on your heavenly stem, your home direction, your lunar mansion and your compatibilities.

The **HORSE** is blessed with extremely fortunate indications with the double *stars of Big Auspicious* and the *Star of Golden Deity* brought by the 24 Mountains Compass of 2021. This sign has great good fortune coming, which should more than make up for the unfortunate stars it had to endure in the last two years. The Horse is an energetic and restless sign full of passion and appetite for adventure, but the last couple of years will have made it difficult for it to pursue its desires. This year changes all of this; the Horse person will feel like a cloud has lifted, and as the year progresses, things get better and better. There are no unlucky indications at all, and the Victory Star #1 promises some very exciting new developments in the Horse's life.

The Horse should boost its fortunes with the **6 Birds Auspicious Multiplier** and benefits from displaying the **Desktop Flag of Victory** in its vicinity.

Desktop Flag of Victory

The **MONKEY** and **ROOSTER** are the signs enjoying the luckiest element luck indications. These two Metal signs have superlative Life Force and Spirit Essence, suggesting an inner determination that is unwavering. These signs know exactly what it is they want and how to go about getting it. Both Monkey and Rooster are known for their innate intelligence and ingenuity, and their already immense brainpower gets a big boost this year. The Monkey in particular enjoys very promising "success" luck; not only can it get what it wants, it receives plenty of recognition to go along with it too!

The **Rooster** can boost success luck by surrounding itself with the presence of the **Victorious Windhorse Carrying a Jewel**, as can the Monkey. Both these signs also have excellent indications from the 24 Mountains, with Monkey enjoying the *Heaven Seal* and Rooster benefitting from the *General Star*. The Monkey should carry the **Dragon Heavenly Seal Amulet** and the Rooster needs the **Ru Yi**.

Dragon
Heavenly
Seal Amulet

The sign that gets hit by the *Five Yellow* this year are the **DRAGON** and **SNAKE**. This indicates that these signs need to watch that the *wu wang* does not bring misfortune their way. The Five Yellow of 2021 sits in a Wood sector, which suggests it is NOT a deadly Five Yellow; nevertheless, the obstacles it brings can cause life to feel very unpleasant indeed and it should be strongly subdued.

Dragon and Snake this year need to carry the **Five Element Pagoda Amulet with Tree of Life** to combat the afflictive energy, turning obstacles into productive challenges, and transforming unfortunate outcomes into promising ones. Both Dragon and Snake are signs that thrive in adversity, gaining strength and shrewdness when the going gets tough. And the *wu wang* of this year can be metamorphosed into positive rather than negative results. The Snake should have the **6 Birds Auspicious Multiplier**, while the Dragon needs the **28 Hums Protection Wheel**.

The WOOD ELEMENT SIGNS of **TIGER** and **RABBIT** both enjoy very good element indications but need to boost success luck with the **Victorious Windhorse** this year. The Tiger benefits from the *Small Auspicious*, and direct access to the hidden wealth of the year, but the Rabbit needs to do more work to boost its prosperity potential. The Tiger should display the **6 Birds Auspicious Multiplier** while the Rabbit MUST carry the **Three Celestial Shields Amulet** to stay protected against the 3 Killings affliction that affects it this year.

The WATER ELEMENT SIGNS of **RAT** and **BOAR** are the most unfortunate in terms of element luck, facing very bad life force and spirit essence. This can cause a sudden lack of confidence in one's own abilities and make these two signs prone to being easily discouraged. What the Rat and Boar need this year are strong cures to lift their inner energies. They need to carry the **Life Force Amulet** and **"Om" Dakini Spirit Enhancing Amulet**. What these two signs do have however are a shared *Big Auspicious Star*. Rat and Boar working together can produce very favourable results, and their affinity with each other gets enhanced this year. These two signs will make good business partners. Of the two, Rat will be luckier than Boar, and should take the lead in any endeavor they embark on together.

The EARTH SIGNS of **OX, DOG, DRAGON** and **SHEEP** all have good life force but bad spirit essence. This suggests that for these signs, they have decent inherent energy, but exposure to the wrong company could be harmful to their mindsets and their motivation levels. They are spiritually weaker than usual and need to carry the **"Om" Dakini Spirit Enhancing Amulet**. Those who are spiritual in nature can draw strength from their belief systems and find solace and comfort in their spiritual practice.

The **SHEEP** meanwhile is also in direct clash with the TAI SUI of the year, and hence the priority for this sign should be to take all steps to appease the God of the Year. The Sheep needs the **Tai Sui Amulet**, and its celestial guardian animal this year should be the **Dragon Pi Yao**. The Sheep can lean on its special friend the Horse, who enjoys superlative luck in 2021. The Sheep working or hanging out with a Horse in the coming year will benefit tremendously from its astrological soulmate. But all four Earth signs are in direct or indirect conflict with the Year God and should thus ALL carry the **Tai Sui Amulet** and have his plaque in the home.

WEALTH LUCK IN 2021

Wealth luck this coming year is weak. It will be difficult to make quick money. Wealth that gets created will come from hard work rather than speculative gains. The year continues to see much disruption to the way business is done, making things difficult for those in sunset industries. Individuals who can spot new opportunities can profit, but increasingly, the free flow of information will reduce the time window for monopolies in new industries. It will be creativity and originality, together with consistent hard work that will allow individuals and businesses to generate income in 2021.

As machines take over more and more jobs, those who do not do something and stubbornly hang on to an old way of life could quickly find themselves being made redundant. The year will not be an easy one for wealth creation, and macro level events continue to depress the immediate outlook.

Certain animal signs will have element luck in their favour when it comes to wealth luck this year; even so, the advice is to weigh all decisions carefully before making them. This is a year when one can take risks, but do not put all your eggs in one basket. Make sure any risks taken are calculated ones backed by understanding and research.

WEALTH ENHANCER: All individuals benefit from inviting in wealth enhancers, particularly the **Asset Wealth Bull** which boosts money and income luck, but also protects against your assets losing value. Those invested in the stock market would benefit greatly from the presence of this bull in the home. It has been designed to look like the stock market bull on Wall Street and carries the meaning "May the market bull for you"; it also features auspicious symbols of good fortune, a red saddle to represent prosperity in 2021, and it is shown presiding over a pile of coins and ingots, signifying its control and dominance over cash. With this bull, you will always have enough money, and even those who sustain losses will quickly make it back.

Asset Wealth Bull

LOVE LUCK IN 2021
SINGLES CAN FIND LOVE IN 2021

For singles, this is a promising year for romance. The *Peach Blossom Star* has settled into the East, a WOOD sector, which gives it strength. The East is also the palace of the Rabbit, which is associated with the Moon and Moon Goddess who presides over fortunes related to love and romance. She bestows wishes to do with relationships, aids in matchmaking soulmates, and improves relations between married couples.

In 2021, the East becomes the place of the "Moon Rabbit" and enhancing this sector manifests love and romance for those looking for true love in their lives. Those wishing to settle down and get married, or searching for their soulmate or one true love, displaying the **Rabbit in the Moon** in the East will manifest this kind of luck for you.

MARRIED COUPLES BEWARE!!!

While there will be plenty of love and romance in 2021, it will not always be the kind that brings happiness. The year's chart also features the *Flower of Romance Star*. Unfortunately, it is the "external" version of this star – making all marriages vulnerable as there will be too much temptation from outside. Innocent flirtations can get out of hand, after-work drinks with colleagues or out-of-town business conferences can lead to inappropriate entanglements, spouses with the seven-year itch could be tempted to act on it. This is a year when those who are married should pay more attention to their other halves.

The *External Star of Romance* often affect those who have grown to take their marriage for granted. As long as you realise it, you can start taking measures to make things right. But what if an affair has already started?

CURE: We advise that when this troublesome star is present, married couples should make an effort to display symbols of marital stability and happiness in the home. All married couples should have the **Marriage Happiness Ducks** in the home, in the SW, East or center. Each can also carry the **Enhancing Relationships Amulet** to protect against third parties elbowing their way in and "crowding" the marriage.

Displaying the **"Rabbit in the Moon" Love Enhancer** in the home is also an excellent protective measure against stars that affect marital peace and happiness. In 2021, all couples can safeguard their marriage by displaying the Moon Rabbit with the full moon in the East part of their home. For those who suspect their spouse is already cheating, you can call on the help of

Kurukulle's
Banner of Love

Kurukulle, the powerful Goddess of Love. Invoking her presence in your life imbues you with her talent for enchantment, giving you your power back when it comes to your spouse and your marriage. You can display her **Banner of Love** or the **Red Tara Home Protection Amulet** – this powerful talisman designed with her image and all her implements of love will repair damage already done to your marriage, while strengthening the bond between you and your spouse. Kurukulle's powers of magnetism will also make it difficult for others to adversely affect your marriage.

We also advise chanting her mantra daily:
OM KURUKULLE HRIH SOHA (21 times or 108 times)

STUDY LUCK IN 2021

To enhance study luck in 2021, students should call on the help of **Manjushri**, the Buddha of Wisdom. Manjushri with his wisdom sword slices through all ignorance in the mind, enhancing one's wisdom and knowledge. Invoking his help benefits not just students and those studying for exams, but also anyone needing to make important decisions and life choices. He clears the mind to make way for effective and efficient accumulation of knowledge – so that "your knowledge is vast, and your understanding complete". This year we have designed a **Manjushri**

Home Amulet for scholars and students to place on their study desk. Manjushri's seed syllable is "DHIH" and chanting this repeatedly in one breath until you run out of breath is the best way to invoke his presence.

You can also chant Manjushri's wisdom mantra:
OM AH RAPA CHA NA DHIH

Make it a habit to chant his mantra either 21 times or 108 times (1 mala) before you sleep each night, or when you can find some quiet time during the day. We suggest you get yourself a **Manjushri Wisdom Mala** which you reserve specially for this purpose – chanting only Manjushri's Wisdom Mantra. This sharpens the mala's power and effectiveness when it comes to study luck, as the energies you direct into the mala as you chant becomes concentrated, making it more and more potent the more you use it.

HEALTH LUCK IN 2021

The Illness Star has flown into the North, the sector of the Rat. This affects all those born in Rat years, but also those whose main doors or bedrooms are located in the North of the home, or those who spend a lot of time in the North sector. Those afflicted with sickness or health problems should have the **Healing Deer** in the North.

Health risks continue to look like a threat going into 2021 so we have designed several potent health and protective talismans to keep everyone safe.

Our **mantra ring** this year features Medicine Buddha's mantra on the outside and Vairocana's mantra on the inside. Medicine Buddha comes to the aid of anyone who is sick and who calls to him for help. Vairocana is the Buddha that protects against contagious diseases. COVID-19 has been a life-altering phenomenon for the whole world throughout the last year, and as we move into 2021, it does not look like things will revert quite back to normal. We need to continue to practise vigilance following new guidelines as they get discovered to keep safe. Mask up, keep your social distance and get used to a new way of living.

The science of feng shui meanwhile always advocates protection before enhancement, so we strongly advise everyone irrespective of their animal sign to always wear or carry health and protective amulets. It can literally save your life!

Medicine
Buddha-
Vairocana
Mantra Ring

The **Medicine Buddha-Vairocana Mantra Ring** is excellent to help keep you safe during these strange times and troubled times.

This year we also strongly recommend the **Health Talisman with Tortoise and Snake**. The Tortoise and Snake are two spiritual creatures associated with longevity, known for their potent powers to heal. The tortoise provides stability both in physical and mental health, while the Snake represents control over the nagas, spirits that can cause ill health and sickness when they are left to their own mischievous devices.

All signs whose element luck tables indicate a poor health category should also place these health cures near to them or carry as portable amulets.

Element Luck of the Rabbit in 2021

Chapter 2

- Metal Rabbit – 10 & 70 years
- Earth Rabbit – 22 & 82 years
- Fire Rabbit – 34 & 94 years
- Wood Rabbit – 46 years
- Water Rabbit – 58 years

ELEMENT LUCK OF THE RABBIT IN 2021

While the Rabbit faces a challenging year ahead, it is helped by its element luck indications. Despite afflictions brought by the 24 mountain winds, the Rabbit enjoys very good life force and good spirit essence, fortifying you against obstacles and allowing you to withstand any difficulties that may be hurled your way.

Success luck indications however are not good, so it is imperative for the Rabbit to work at raising its personal *lung ta* – the best way to do this is with the **Victorious Windhorse Carrying a Jewel**. Place anywhere on your desk, and carry a Windhorse with you wherever you go. You otherwise have a promising element luck chart, so it is important to fix this shortfall in your luck this year.

2021 will see Rabbits remain steadfast and confident in their abilities despite whatever else may be going on outside of their control. As personalities, Rabbits are the ultimate diplomats, able to navigate difficult situations with their inborn empathy and understanding. This year you will need to harness these diplomatic skills to a greater extent, and it will be Rabbits with the most tact who will win others onto their side to help them with their causes.

ELEMENT LUCK OF

	EARTH RABBIT 82/22 years	METAL RABBIT 70/10 years	WATER RABBIT 58 years
Life Force	very good	very good	very good
Health	good	very good	excellent
Wealth	**neutral**	bad	excellent
Success	very bad	very bad	very bad
Spirit Essence	very good	very good	very good

THE RABBIT IN 2021

WOOD RABBIT 46 years	FIRE RABBIT 34 years	2021 Element
very good ☺☺	very good ☺☺	Earth
very bad xx	neutral ox	Earth
very bad xx	very good ☺☺	Metal
very bad xx	very bad xx	Water
very good ☺☺	very good ☺☺	Fire

Indeed, the Rabbit's biggest advantage this year will be your army of friends and allies. While your personal fortunes may be afflicted, you do have the luck of the Peach Blossom Star, which boosts the quality of all relationships and makes others want to help you. Don't sabotage yourself by pushing help away when it is offered. This is a year when the Rabbit that thrives is the one that is surrounded by friends and supporters.

Spiritually you are strong, so you are unlikely to succumb to giving up when the going gets tough. But when obstacles crop up, tapping the brains of others may help you find your way out of a bind more quickly than trying to figure things out on your own.

All Rabbits should give their friendship luck a boost with the **Friendship Amulet**. Put more effort into nurturing your relationships, something not difficult for this sign as you are by nature a sociable animal. Catch up with old friends and follow up with new ones. This is a year when you can build lifelong friendships and rekindle long lost comradeships. Looking to the past may not be a bad thing this year when it comes to seeking out allies.

WEALTH LUCK FOR
THE DIFFERENT RABBITS

Wealth luck differs for the different element Rabbits, but especially benefits the **58-year-old Water Rabbit** and the **34-year-old Wood Rabbit** this year. These two Rabbits enjoy excellent element wealth luck, which suggests that financially, you will be very comfortable this year and your wealth can grow. To take fullest advantage of this, you should display the **Tree Bringing 3 Kinds of Wealth** in your living space; this will add growth energy to your wealth potential, boosting investment luck, and for some of you, even attract a windfall.

The **70-year-old Metal Rabbit** has a less robust indication in the wealth luck category, so the advice for this Rabbit is to steer clear of risky investments this year. For you, the best strategy is to ensure you maintain a sufficiently diversified portfolio and do not succumb to taking financial risks, no matter how irresistible, as luck is not on your side with wealth prospects this year.

The **46-year-old Wood Rabbit** has its wealth category at a very bad level, so this is a warning to take steps to preserve your wealth. Avoid risky plays when it comes to money matters. If you have your children's education to think about, you may want to start building your nest egg. This is not the year for frivolous expenditures. Unexpected and unavoidable expenses could crop up, disrupting your personal financial plan for the year. Make adjustments as needed and stay frugal this year. This Rabbit needs the **"Hum" Dakini Wealth Protection Amulet** to safeguard its wealth.

HEALTH OF THE RABBIT

The only Rabbit with anything serious to worry about when it comes to health this year is the **46-year-old Wood Rabbit**. For this Rabbit, you should pay more attention to this aspect of your life. Go for your regular check-ups. If you don't feel well for any reason, get it looked at. The advice is not to leave health concerns to a point where it is too late to do something about it. For the 46-year-old Rabbit, we recommened that you carry or wear **Health Amulets** at all times and have the **Medicine Buddha and 7 Sugatas Gau** near you.

The Rabbit's element luck in 2021 indicates a strong sense of purpose but a lack of success luck. Your biggest advantage this year will come from having good friends on your side.

Nurture your relationships and don't take your pals for granted; you're going to need their help at some point this year!

METAL RABBIT 10 year old	
life force	very good oo
health	very good oo
wealth	bad x
success	very bad xx
spirit essence	very good oo

THE 10-YEAR-OLD METAL RABBIT

The Rabbit child is often a delight to handle. They are easy-going, polite and able to follow rules. They are a pleasure to teach and a delight to parent. They have little trouble finding their own friends and fitting in at school. This year, as the young Rabbit leaves the single digits and turns 10, he or she starts becoming more self-assured than ever. His or her talents become more obvious, and as a parent to a Rabbit child, it is easy to bring up a Rabbit as this sign will know exactly what he or she wants. There is no need to push them to try their hand at a multitude of extracurricular activities – they will pick and choose for themselves, then bug you for lessons!

2021 for the young Rabbit is a preparation year. Success luck needs boosting but good progress can be made. Do not set milestones too high. Formulate goals with a number of smaller stepping-stones along the way; this is the best way to keep this young

Rabbit motivated. If the young Rabbit stays focused, there will be some serious skills developed by the end of this year.

For the parent to a Rabbit child, pay close attention to your child's interests. For all the self-sufficiency and independence of this sign, the young Rabbit nevertheless thrives on praise from their parents and teachers, which will go a long way to boosting its confidence and staying power.

Friendships feature heavily in the young Rabbit's life this year, and young pals pursuing a common shared interest will add much to this Rabbit's progress.

Parents to a Rabbit child should help enable the kinds of friendships that facilitate this positive interaction and reinforcement. The young Rabbit thrives on mixing with similarly minded and ambitious peers. They need their friends as much as they need their parents and authority figures.

Try not to helicopter-parent your Rabbit child too much, as this will hamper the young Rabbit's own innate curiosity and creativity. Instead, set the stage and let them romp to their own heart's content – you'll be impressed by what your young charge can dig up!

The best amulet for the 10-year-old Rabbit is the **Manjushri Gau** featuring the Buddha of Wisdom. This will draw out its many natural talents and ensure they thrive to their fullest potential in a year when it also enjoys the Scholastic Star. Place on their study desk. This Rabbit also benefits from the **Manjushri "Dhih" Scholastic Amulet**.

EARTH RABBIT 22 year old	
life force	very good GG
health	good G
wealth	neutral ox
success	very bad xx
spirit essence	very good GG

THE 22-YEAR-OLD EARTH RABBIT

The **22-year-old Earth Rabbit** still in college should focus on conscientious work to get through the year. Success luck should be boosted with the **Victorious Windhorse Carrying a Jewel** nearby, but there will be no success without the work put in. This is not a year when talent alone will work; it will be your effort that will win you the accolades you are looking for.

Resist being hasty in your decision-making; you may change your mind several times before deciding on which paths to take. There is no need to rush headlong into anything, and in a year like this one, it is better to have mulled over all your than be too impulsive in your decisions.

For the Rabbit sign, this is a year when success luck is limited, so be sure you are financially secure before taking risk-it-all decisions. If choosing between looking for a job or striking out on your own, make the sensible choice.

This Rabbit likes the finer things in life, but this is a year when you may have to wake up to some realities. Some of you may feel the instant poverty when your educational career comes to an end and you have to start fending for yourself. But the Rabbit sign adapts easily, so while you may feel out of sorts in the adjustment period, things will not become dire.

Wealth luck is neutral – neither good nor bad. Your Earth heavenly stem will ensure you keep your feet on the ground even if your mind may be elsewhere.

The Fire Rabbit benefits from the **Dragon Tortoise** if career success is what you are after. Wealth luck for you is promising and can be boosted with the **Ox Finding Hidden Gold**. Your success luck is however lacking; carry the **Windhorse Success Amulet** to improve this aspect of your luck.

FIRE RABBIT 34 year old	
life force	very good ᏀᏀ
health	**neutral** Ꮻᚷ
wealth	very good ᏀᏀ
success	very bad ᏒᏒ
spirit essence	very good ᏀᏀ

THE 34-YEAR-OLD FIRE RABBIT

This Rabbit has wealth luck on its side this year. While success luck may be lacking, you have few financial worries and you could be in for some monetary promotion or windfall. The entrepreneurs among you will see business improve this year. For this Rabbit, you are in the prime of your life and in the right place to pursue whatever ambition you so desire. Your strong life force will be a big asset to you, although this is not the year to be taking risks that are too big.

As you are still young it makes sense to pursue different interests. You have many paths open to you, and this is a year when you will have the luxury to pick and choose. The pitfalls will be bearable, and the end results can be good. Look on everything you do as part of a learning experience, so even if the results in the near term are not what you hoped for, if you keep on track, you will eventually get there.

The Fire Rabbit's secret weapon is your ability and willingness to try things. You are easy-going and you never allow anything to upset you too much. This gives you a thick skin and a resilience to what others think, an invaluable trait especially when success is not immediate. Your Fire heavenly stem makes you deftly charming. You find it easy to bend others over to your will through your sheer skills of diplomacy. This year this talent will come in especially useful, as the more people you have on your side, the better your chances of achieving what you are hoping to.

This Rabbit benefits from the **Luo Han sitting on Dragon Tortoise** if career success is what you are after. Carry the **Asset Wealth Bull Talisman** to make the most of your promising wealth luck in 2021.

WOOD RABBIT 46 year old	
life force	very good OO
health	very bad xx
wealth	very bad xx
success	very bad xx
spirit essence	very good OO

THE 46-YEAR-OLD WOOD RABBIT

This Rabbit needs to lie low this year. Of all your Rabbit siblings, you are unfortunately the most afflicted in terms of element luck, with a "very bad" showing in your health, wealth and success categories. Thankfully, you have good life force and spirit essence levels, which strengthens your character enabling you to overcome more obstacles and more disappointments. Remember that every "failure" along the way is an opportunity to learn, and Rabbit people thrive on such learning opportunities.

This Rabbit, while outwardly docile and diplomatic, secretly thrives on drama and commotion, so when life becomes too easy-going, you actually start to wither. But give you a challenge or even a crisis and it awakens your every fibre. 2021 promises to be an eventful year with numerous trials and tests, but you fight each one with your characteristic resilience and emerge stronger and psychically more fulfilled.

While this is not the year when you can expect to make big money, or enjoy anything you can call commercial success, your life will be extremely rewarding when it comes to friendships and relationships. While attainment luck may not be great, you have excellent relationship luck, and those who want it, romantic luck also.

This Rabbit needs to give a boost to your poor wealth showing – for this we recommend installing **Wealth Cabinets** in the West. This is a potent symbol representing wealth that continues to augment and grow, ensuring your investments do not suffer, and that you always have enough for a rainy day. You should also carry your money in this year's **Red Wealth Wallet**. For those invested in the stock market, you benefit very much from the **Asset Wealth Bull**.

WATER RABBIT 58 year old	
life force	very good GG
health	excellent GGG
wealth	excellent GGG
success	very bad xx
spirit essence	very good GG

THE 58-YEAR-OLD WATER RABBIT

A fabulous year awaits the 58-year-old Water Rabbit. For you, the year ahead is not just rewarding from a monetary point of view, there is also plenty of personal happiness in store! You enjoy excellent indications in your wealth and health categories along with your strong personal energy categories. This is a year when everything connected to making money enjoys favourable luck. You take new directions in your business without risk of losing money. You can pursue any kind of aspiration you desire.

The Water Rabbit is a highly excitable sign, much more so than your other Rabbit siblings. You are more akin to the wild hare than the domesticated rabbit and are happiest when given free rein to roam the ends of the earth. You are a romantic at heart and will fall for anyone who knows how to romance you right. Even at your age, you maintain your passionate ways. 2021's *Flower of Romances star* may well fall upon you, rekindling a flame that has gone dim over the years, or even bring a new love into your life.

Commercially, this is a highly fruitful year for you, which continues on from last year's run of good luck. You also enjoy excellent health luck, so you have little to worry about here. Your energy levels are robust, and coupled with your good wealth luck, those thinking of venturing into a new business or going into partnership with a friend can try your luck in endeavors that catch your fancy. You need to be serious about making investments and to avoid being frivolous, but you can be encouraged by the wonderful energies that are working in your favour. What you have this year will bring you exceptional luck, so the advice is to live this year to the fullest!

For this Rabbit, we recommend the **8 Auspicious Objects Ru Yi**. This scepter of power will ensure that all the good fortune due to you this year comes within easy reach. Because your *lung ta* is low, you need this year's Windhorse, **Victorious Windhorse Carrying a Jewel.** Also display the **Desktop Flag of Victory** on your desk.

Desktop Flag of Victory

METAL RABBIT 70 year old	
life force	very good GG
health	very good GG
wealth	bad x
success	very bad xx
spirit essence	very good GG

THE 70-YEAR-OLD METAL RABBIT

This Rabbit enjoys strong health luck, so you are physically fit and well, but wealth luck is not so promising. This suggests that this is a year to enjoy life and not take making money so seriously. It is a year to enjoy an easier and slower moving pace. Looking towards spiritual development holds out the most promise. You can stimulate your mind by indulging in new interests, taking up a new hobby or adopting a new cause.

The Metal Rabbit has always known how to live well, and this year will be no exception. This is a year to slow down and savour all that life has to offer. Take your mind off financial pursuits, and instead, turn your efforts towards refined pastimes and diversions

such as painting, music and the arts. Because your luck in commercial ventures is limited this year, it is best to refrain from being too heavily involved in business and investment pursuits, but you are also prone to restlessness if not sufficiently stimulated, so while you may leave financial pursuits to the younger generation, there is no need to retire completely. Find something else to fill your time. This Rabbit does not thrive when lazing about doing nothing. Find a charity, society or something to direct your abundant energy towards this year.

This Metal Rabbit benefits from the **Ox Finding Hidden Gold**. This will boost your low levels of element wealth luck and help you ink out a good living despite less than promising indications. You can also carry the **Income Generating Amulet**. For success luck, carry the **Windhorse Success Amulet**.

EARTH RABBIT 82 year old	
life force	very good ဂဂ
health	good ဂ
wealth	**neutral** ox
success	very bad xx
spirit essence	very good ဂဂ

THE 82-YEAR-OLD EARTH RABBIT

The 82-year-old Earth Rabbit has a very decent element luck chart. At your age, when you enjoy good health, everything else falls into place, and in 2021, your health luck looks good. Wealth luck is at a neutral level, suggesting that while you won't run into money problems, it is not a year when you will find it easy to accumulate a lot of new wealth. What you should aim for is preservation of what you have already made. Display a **Yellow Wealth Cabinet** in your home sector of East and place the **Asset Wealth Bull** in the West sector to activate the prosperity star there.

In 2021, you need to guard against taking big financial risks. Going out on a limb can bring distressing results and you do not want to upset yourself unnecessarily. There are benefits to doing little in terms of making decisions that require knowledge of the investment markets. It i would suit you better to adpot a more easygoing lifestyle at home and leaving these decisions to the younger generation.

Those who enjoy spiritual retreats with like-minded people can consider going for a retreat to engage your spiritual dimensions. This can bring wonderful satisfaction and could open new worlds to you. Being on retreat enables you to rest your mind in a natural way. You do not stop thinking, but you think in a way that heals your inner soul.

This Rabbit should wear the **Medicine Buddha - Vairocana Mantra Ring** for good health and long life.

Four Pillars Chart 2021

Chapter 3

FOUR PILLARS CHART 2021

An important indicator of the potential of any year is the Four Pillars chart of the year. This reveals the impact of the five elements of the year. When all five elements are present, it indicates a balance, a preferred situation. In feng shui, we are always striving for balance, and when something is out of balance, we always endeavor to bring things back into balance by introducing the missing element. This year, the chart

HOUR	DAY	MONTH	YEAR
壬 Yang Water	癸 Yin Water	庚 Yang Metal	辛 Yin Metal
壬子 Yang Water Rat	己未 Yin Earth Sheep	甲寅 Yang Wood Tiger	己丑 Yin Earth Ox

This year's Four Pillars chart lacks Fire, the element that signifies wealth luck.

is obviously missing Fire, the element that indicates WEALTH LUCK, so the year lacks opportunities to make money.

However, the eight characters in the Four Pillars – made up of 4 heavenly stems and 4 earthly branches – are not the only elements present. The interaction of these elements, depending on where and how they are positioned within the chart, generates a set of hidden elements as well as special stars. We use this chapter to analyse each part of this year's Four Pillars chart, and mention the most significant findings.

2021's Paht Chee chart indicates a strong self-element of Water, which boosts competitive energies and puts everyone on edge. Friends become foes when the stakes are raised, so this is a year to constantly watch one's back. The year's chart is unbalanced; it is missing the vital element of FIRE, which represents wealth and financial success. It is thus a year when it will be difficult to make much headway in the creation of new wealth. Profits may take a long time to get realized and there are few speculative gains to be made.

Prosperity comes with hard work rather than with a stroke of luck. This is definitely not a year to strike it rich via the lottery.

Here is a closer look at the most important indications this year:

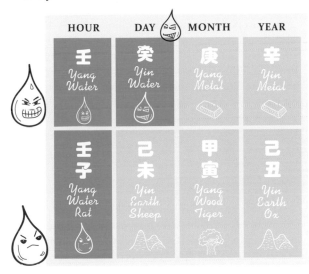

HOUR	DAY	MONTH	YEAR
壬	癸	庚	辛
Yang Water	Yin Water	Yang Metal	Yin Metal
壬 子	己 未	甲 寅	己 丑
Yang Water Rat	Yin Earth Sheep	Yang Wood Tiger	Yin Earth Ox

There appears to be way too much Water in this year's chart.

A YEAR OF STRONG WATER
indicating a competitive year

First, the self-element of the year is Strong Water. It is a year when rivalry becomes enhanced and when politics can get unscrupulous. Watch your back and reserve your trust for your very innermost circle. Indeed, even your inner circle could let you down if the circumstances dictate. Betrayals happen of their own accord, sometimes without the guilty party's conscious intention. Learn to forgive and move on but protect yourself by being more careful and by putting safeguards in place. Remove temptation where you can and stay close to all you are working with.

 PROTECTION: Those in business are advised to carry the **Kuan Kung on Horseback Anti-Betrayal Amulet**. This will protect you against the betrayal of others and being let down by people whom you trust. It keeps you prepared for whatever the winds and waters bring your way.

For the Rabbit-born to get your timing right for all your moves and decisions, we suggest keeping the **"Green Dragon" Constellation Lucky Charms** near you. Comprising the 7 Sky Animals of the Dragon Constellation, these will ensure you act at just the right time for outcomes to turn out always positively for you.

In any competitive endeavour, it could well feel like a fight to the death. Diplomatic compromises will be difficult to achieve, and different factions and interest groups find it harder to reach win-win scenarios. But

it is nevertheless important to try. Sometimes being
the bigger person will help; but recognize when you
have to fight and when you don't. Indeed, do
not mistakenly think you are in fact being
the magnanimous one when you are being
taken for a fool. It is a year when it is prudent
to carry protection always. The **28 Hums
Protection Amulet** is an excellent all-round
amulet that will safeguard you from all
kinds of harm.

SOLUTION: The excess of Water energy in the
chart needs to be resolved. Use **WOOD energy**
to weaken the excess Water. Having plenty of
greenery and live plants in your living space will
help re-balance the energies and will also bring
vital growth energy to a year which lacks the
presence of the *Lap Chun*, or "Spring".

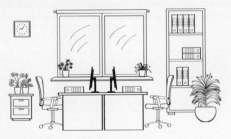

This year, having plenty of plants and Wood energy
in the home around you will help soak up the excess
Water in the year's chart.

BALANCE OF YIN & YANG

Second, there are two Yang pillars and two Yin Pillars. There is thus a good mix between energetic periods and restive ones, with no dominance of work over play, or vice versa. The Yang Month and Hour Pillars bring great vitality, while the Yin Year and Day Pillars bring balance. There should be more than enough strength to propel positive chi forward and upward. People in general are open to different viewpoints. If negative energies can be kept under control and sufficiently subdued, the year is then able to propel forward, benefitting many.

This year there is good balance between Yang and Yin in the year's Four Pillars chart.

CLASH OF SHEEP WITH OX
indicating strong conflict energy

Third, there is a clash of SHEEP with OX in the Earth Branches. This clash between two Earth animals suggests that the clash will be between leaders. Earth is the element that represents leadership and rank, thus animosity will likely be between those who are in charge. But because those in power are especially strong this year, fighting can become ferocious, with the damage dealt far-reaching. There will be strong clashes between the leaders of nations.

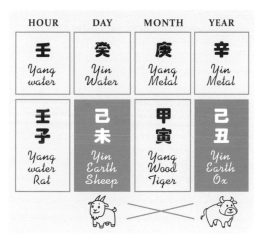

HOUR	DAY	MONTH	YEAR
壬 Yang water	癸 Yin Water	庚 Yang Metal	辛 Yin Metal
壬子 Yang water Rat	己未 Yin Earth Sheep	甲寅 Yang Wood Tiger	己丑 Yin Earth Ox

The clash between Ox and Sheep brings many problems to the year, especially between those who are in charge and everyone else, who could end up as collateral damage.

Within family units, because the clash occurs in the Day Pillar, there is likely to be strong conflict between spouses.

SOLUTION: There may be more marital problems in 2021 with the Sheep in the Self-Spouse pillar clashing with the Year pillar. In the family unit, this coupled with the presence of the *External Flower of Romance* star brings all kinds of problems to husband and wife. Every home this year should have the **"Rabbit in the Moon" Love Enhancer** and better still if both husband and wife carry the **Enhancing Relationships Amulet**. Recognize when an outsider is trying to make trouble in your marriage, and refrain from siding with a third party over your spouse, no matter how much your husband or wife may be annoying you. When you allow an outsider into the mix, this year, such troubles can escalate very quickly.

Enhancing
Relationships Amulet

SPECIAL LINK BETWEEN RAT & OX
bringing creativity and inventiveness

Fourth, there is however a very strong affinity between RAT and OX in the Earthly Branches of the Year and Hour Pillar. This is a heaven sent because it serves to repair some of the damage resulting from the Ox-Sheep clash. The Year Pillar of the Ox forms a soulmate pairing with the Hour Pillar of the Rat, which means there is a good beginning and a good ending to the year, what the Chinese refer to as having a head and tail, a suggestion that things that

The Rat and Ox in this year's chart form a very special affinity, bringing relationship and completion luck.

get started have a good chance to reach satisfactory completion. The two signs of Rat and Ox are extremely harmonious together, generating the *House of Cleverness and Creativity*, with the Rat starting and the Ox completing. This endows the year with wonderful ingenuity and inventiveness.

The presence of the Rat & Ox in the year's Four Pillars suggests a year when true friendship means something.

These two signs are also a secret-friend pair, indicating **good friendship luck** through the year. While there are indications of strong competition and rivalry, there is also much potential for firm friendships, and opportunities for friends to demonstrate their loyalties and allegiance. A year perhaps of finding out who one's true friends are.

ENHANCER: Get the **"Perfect Partnerships to Attract Big Wealth" Enhancer**. This enhancer featuring the Ox and Rat will boost all the positive indications of this combination. Display in a prominent area in the home; in the living room, or near the dining room where you spend a lot of time. The number "8" on the Ox activates for the missing wealth luck of the year.

NO PROSPERITY LUCK INDICATED
... but there is hidden wealth

Fifth, there is MISSING WEALTH. Fire which represents wealth is completely missing from the main chart. What this indicates is that it will be difficult to make money. New businesses will take time getting off the ground, sales will be slow, industries that are shrinking will continue to do so, while their replacements will take time to take flight. Profit margins get squeezed as information becomes more and more freely available, and technology continues to disrupt at breakneck pace. This year, if one wants to stay afloat, it is vitally important to keep up with the world that is so rapidly changing around us.

While there will be results and completions, it will nevertheless feel like an interim year, because we are at the beginning end of a new cycle, and not quite at the close of the current period. 2021 represents the second animal sign of the cycle after the new decade last year opened with the Rat, and we are heading towards the end of Period 8, and the beginning of Period 9, but we are not quite there yet.

There is a lack of obvious wealth in 2021, but those who look harder can find gold. This year, there is HIDDEN WEALTH brought by the sign of the TIGER.

While WEALTH luck may be lacking, there is however HIDDEN WEALTH brought by the TIGER. This will bring some respite, and keep us tided over, but it is wealth that comes in its own time rather than overnight. What this means is that 2021 is a year when we can lay the foundations for future wealth, but we must not get our hopes up for immediate results.

That the hidden wealth star is brought by the Tiger bodes well for friends of the Tiger – the Dog and especially the Horse.

The Dog enjoys one *Small Auspicious Star* from the 24 mountains chart, while the Horse enjoys not one but *TWO Big Auspicious Stars,* together with a *Golden Deity Star*. These two astrological allies of the big cat are lucky in this respect in terms of money-making prospects, although all signs can boost wealth luck with suitable activators and enhancers.

THE COLOUR FOR WEALTH: The wearing of the most auspicious colour of the spectrum RED will bring significant added benefits in 2021. Red is the colour which represents ultimate YANG, which serves to boost the year's vitality, but will do double duty in enhancing the missing Wealth element of the year. Red in 2021 stands for WEALTH, so wearing this colour as part of your wardrobe or accessories will give you a

For Wealth

boost of good fortune. You should also carry the **"Increase Your Wealth Luck" Gold Talisman Card** featuring the God of Wealth Tsai Shen Yeh seated on a Tiger. This will attract wealth of the kind that keeps increasing and will help you tap the hidden wealth luck of the year.

You can also display the **Bejewelled God of Wealth sitting on a Tiger** in figurine form in the home.

Bejewelled God of
Wealth sitting on a Tiger

Before the New Year arrives, make sure you get our specially created **Red Wealth Wallet** featuring the Wealth Ox. It is auspicious each year to change to a new wallet and especially lucky to take some money from your old wallet and transfer it over to your new wallet. Doing so for this year will ensure you take some of the energy of last year, and carry it over into the following year. In 2021 you definitely want to do this, as the previous Year of the Rat carried two *Lap Chuns*, or two "Springs" while this year has none.

Keep the lights in your home brightly turned on throughout the year, especially in the WEST sector, which plays host to the Prosperity Star #8.

POWERFUL SPIRITUAL ENHANCER: For wealth luck that is potent and long-lasting, an excellent ritual to incorporate into your life is the **White Dzambala Ritual**. Invite in **White Dzambala and the Four Dakinis** who pull in

wealth from the four directions. Display in a
respectful place in the home and recite White
Dzambala's mantra as regularly as you can.

White Dzambala's Mantra:
*Om Padma Krodha Arya Dzambala
Hridaya Hum Phat*

When you gaze upon him and chant his mantra
regularly, he manifests great riches in your life
and attracts incredible opportunities that can
bring wealth of a big meaningful and lasting
kind.

INVITE IN THE ROOSTER: The Rooster brings
the #8 Wealth Star in 2021, so it is extremely
auspicious to have many images of Roosters
in the home this year. The
Rooster is also the symbol that
ensures politicking is kept to a
minimum, protecting against
harmful gossip and slander.
The Rooster is also wonderful
for protecting the marriage,
preventing any troublesome third
party from trying to come between
husband and wife.

Rooster
with
Crown

There are many benefits to displaying the Rooster this year; indeed, it may be a good time to start collecting Roosters, made of different colours and in different materials if you wish. You can also display Rooster Art in the home, which is most auspicious. Display in the West part of the home.

Our new **Rooster with Crown** this year has been embellished with powerful symbols of protection and good fortune, to ensure the negative energies of the year cannot harm you. It features the "Anti Evil-Eye" to protect against jealousy, the Double Dorje for wisdom in decision making and the powerful "Hum" seed syllable for strong protection. Its powerful feathers sweep away all harmful energies and its crown symbolizes holding dominion over the year.

LUCKY SPECIAL STARS OF 2021

Sixth, there are two potentially VERY AUSPICIOUS stars in the year's Four Pillars chart. These are seriously good stars noted for being strong and very explicit in their beneficial influence. These stars have the capability of bringing incredible good fortune to those who know how to activate them correctly, while making sure the positive aspects of their influences materialize.

These stars impact different animal signs differently and in varying degrees, but are nevertheless very beneficial for all signs. Note that you will need to wear or carry the relevant activators to ensure that you make the most of the positive influence of these stars.

THE STAR OF PROSPECTS
brings many new opportunities

This star brought by the Earthly Branch of Rat in the Hour Pillar with the self-element of Water indicates many new opportunities in the coming year. This favourable star conjures up a very special energy that rewards determination and staying power, resonating

HOUR	DAY	MONTH	YEAR
壬 Yang Water	癸 Yin Water	庚 Yang Metal	辛 Yin Metal
壬子 Yang Water Rat	己未 Yin Earth Sheep	甲寅 Yang Wood Tiger	己丑 Yin Earth Ox

The Star of Prospects brings many new opportunities in the coming year.

with the Ox sign of the year, a reminder that those who retain their passion for success will benefit from its presence. This star suggests there is nothing that cannot be achieved for those prepared to work hard. The more ambitious one is, the further one can go this year.

STAR OF PROSPECTS: To activate this star in your favour, keep an **image of an Ox** near you. We suggest the **Asset Wealth Bull** to magnify wealth luck and to ensure the hard work you put in meets with proportionate success. This bull has been designed with an auspicious saddle in red, the colour that signifies wealth in 2021, wearing a harness of coins and stepping on a pile of wealth and ingots, symbolizing the accumulation of assets.

This beautiful enhancer will allow you to accumulate everything you work for and ensure you do not spend everything you earn. It will also increase the opportunities that come your way.

THE STAR OF POWERFUL MENTORS
brings Benefactor Luck

The Star of Powerful Mentors which was also in last year's chart makes another appearance in 2021. This star is brought by the OX in the Year Pillar and the Heavenly Stem of YANG METAL in the Month Pillar. This star is especially beneficial for the younger generation, who have the auspicious luck of influential people turning up in their lives to help them, giving them meaningful advice and powerful support.

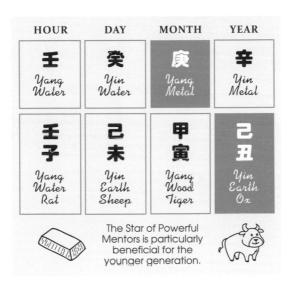

HOUR	DAY	MONTH	YEAR
壬 Yang Water	癸 Yin Water	庚 Yang Metal	辛 Yin Metal
壬子 Yang Water Rat	己未 Yin Earth Sheep	甲寅 Yang Wood Tiger	己丑 Yin Earth Ox

The Star of Powerful Mentors is particularly beneficial for the younger generation.

For students hungry for success, mentors will open doors to scholarship, and teachers will provide fabulous inspiration and motivation. Opportunities abound and there will be unseen hands supporting you. Those just starting out in your careers can find a mentor figure to guide you and to show you the ropes. An influential boss could fast-track your promotion up the ranks.

ACTIVATE THE STAR OF POWERFUL MENTORS: Bring this star to life by displaying **Kuan Kung** in the home. You can also display near to you work or study desk. Another powerful activator for this star is the **Nobleman Qui Ren Talisman**. The

benefits of this special star are immense, so it is worth activating. It brings help from the heavens, manifesting someone in your life with the wish and means to help you, and ensures those with this kind of power stay firmly on your side.

AFFLICTIVE STARS OF 2021

There are two unlucky stars brought by the Four Pillars chart of the year. These, when not attended to with relevant cures, can wreak a lot of havoc and create a lot of misfortune, but their ill influence can be avoided if you take special note and address them.

THE AGGRESSIVE SWORD STAR
is a Double-Edged Sword

The Aggressive Sword Star formed by the Yin Water in the Heavenly Stem of the Day Pillar and the Earthly Branch of Ox in the Year Pillar suggests a year of

HOUR	DAY	MONTH	YEAR
壬 Yang Water	癸 Yin Water	庚 Yang Metal	辛 Yin Metal
壬子 Yang Water Rat	己未 Yin Earth Sheep	甲寅 Yang Wood Tiger	己丑 Yin Earth Ox

The Aggressive Sword Star can be both good and bad.

intense aggression. It indicates the strengthening
of the underdog's chi, so it points to a rise of
revolutionary fervour, people revolting against
authority. Strikes continue, spawning groups around
the globe to walk similar paths. Protests advocating
for greater equality, non-discrimination, fighting
against police brutality and other social injustices
continue to pick up steam. There will be anger,
passion, rioting and violence.

At its pinnacle, the presence of this star suggests the
emergence of powerful leaders on opposing sides, or
of highly influential opposition to established leaders.
It suggests the rise of a people who seize power
by fair means or foul. The name of this star is **Yang
Ren**, which describes *"yang essence sharp blade that
inflicts damage"*. This is a star with great potential for
either very good or very bad influences to materialize
during the year, although generally, the influence
tends to be more negative than positive. There is risk
of revolution and of the toppling of unpopular leaders
in power.

> The Aggressive Sword Star brings
> potential for violence & bloodshed. This
> star must be strongly subdued.

In this year's chart, the *Star of Aggressive Sword* is
created by the strong YIN WATER of the DAY pillar,

with the presence of the OX in the YEAR pillar. Here, note that the WATER element is strong in the chart, making the presence of the Aggressive Sword much more negative. It indicates that those emerging as leaders for the underdog in 2021 will end up being heavy-handed and quick-tempered. They may be charismatic but will also be strong-willed, conceited, arrogant, overbearing and self-centered - all nasty traits that spell the potential for bloodshed and violence wherever they emerge. There is real danger of this this year!

CURE: To shield against the harmful effects of the Aggressive Sword Star, the best remedy is a powerful spiritual Stupa. The **Kumbum Stupa** is especially beneficial as it contains one hundred holy images, invoking the protection of all the world's Wisdom Protectors. This Stupa will ensure that all family members living within the home stay protected against aggression or violence of any kind. It is also a good idea to carry the **28 Hums Protection Wheel Amulet** at all times.

Kumbum Stupa

THE FLOWER OF ROMANCE STAR (EXTERNAL) *makes marriages vulnerable*

This star is sometimes confused with the *Peach Blossom Star* because it addresses the destiny of love; but while both influence love and romance, they are very different in their effects. When the Flower of Romance is present, it suggests love blossoms easily, but it is not the kind of love that leads to marriage and family. It indicates instead the possibility of extramarital affairs, bringing stress and unhappiness to married couples. There is also a difference between *internal* and *external romance*, and in this year of the Ox, it is unfortunately the latter that prevails. So the year

HOUR	DAY	MONTH	YEAR
壬	癸	庚	辛
Yang Water	Yin Water	Yang Metal	Yin Metal
壬 子	己 未	甲 寅	己 丑
Yang Water Rat	Yin Earth Sheep	Yang Wood Tiger	Yin Earth Ox

The External Flower of Romance Star brings stress and risk of infidelity to marriages.

is likely to see increased occurrences of infidelity and break-ups of marriages.

Marriages are vulnerable to the External Flower of Romance this year.

The SHEEP in the Day Pillar and RAT of the Hour Pillar indicate the presence of the *External Romance Star*, making all marriages vulnerable to straying by husband OR wife. Things are made worse as the Sheep clashes with the ruling animal of the year, the Ox. This causes misunderstandings between couples, and danger of an outsider fanning the flames from the side.

FIXING THE EXTERNAL STAR OF ROMANCE: To prevent this affliction from doing real harm to your marriage, carry the **Enhancing Relationships Amulet**, especially if you suspect your spouse already has eyes for someone outside your marriage. Or if you are constantly fighting with each other, or forced into a situation when you have to spend large amounts of time apart (e.g. if one of you commutes to a different country for work, or travel a lot for work). It is also a good idea to display a pair of **Marriage Happiness Ducks** in the SW of the home, or if you suspect something has already started, place an **Amethyst Geode** tied with red string under the foot of the bed of the straying partner.

You can also invite in the **image of an Ox and Horse** to counter the affliction. This subdues the possibility of infidelity causing problems for you. The OX/HORSE presence will create a special "cross" with the SHEEP/RAT affliction.

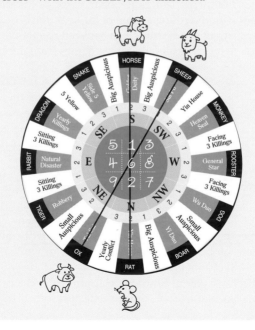

Flying Stars of 2021
Chapter 4

FLYING STAR CHART OF 2021
Heavenly Star *rules the year*

The Flying Star chart on first glance is a big improvement on last year's chart. The Loss Star #7 of 2020 makes way for the *Heaven Star* #6 in this Year of the Ox 2021. The Heaven Star becomes the dominant star of this year. This white star is associated with many good things, attracting the celestial luck of the heavens and providing the unseen hand of opportunity and guidance from above. Everyone stands to benefit from this star, especially if the center of the home where the star is located is kept well-energized and active throughout the year.

In 2021, it benefits to keep the center of the home very active! Have friends over & use this space well.

Rearrange your furniture so you naturally gravitate to the center of your home. The more you include this space in daily usage, the better the luck of the whole family for this coming year.

2021's chart suits homes with open plan layouts arranged around the center part of the home. This is where the luck of auspicious heaven energy congregates this year, and keeping this part of the home lively and vibrant with lots of music, chatter and activity will serve to "activate" this star, bringing it to life!

Work at repositioning your furniture and seating if you have to. This year it is extremely auspicious for all members of the household to spend plenty of time in the center sector, and when you have guests, entertain them in this part of the home. If your home has a piano, place it in the center so every time someone sits down to play it, the sector gets energized.

If your home is not an open-concept one, keep the doors to the center room in the home ajar as much as possible.

You want the energy that emanates from the center to seep into all other areas of the home. The more you energize this part of your house, and the more you suppress the bad luck sectors, the better the luck of the whole household for the year.

ENHANCE THE CENTER GRID
with the Celestial Water Dragon

This year, every household benefits from the presence of the **Celestial Water Dragon**. Place this celestial creature in the center of your home and of your office. The celestial Dragon is the ultimate symbol of good fortune and its deep blue colour and cloud imagery suggest its heavenly origins. This Dragon is auspicious wherever he is displayed, but this year he especially benefits the center part of the home, which houses the Heaven Star #6.

The Celestial Water Dragon is the best enhancer for the #6 Heaven Star which occupies the central sector in 2021.

Placing the Celestial Dragon here will attract plenty of new and lucrative opportunities into your life, as well as the patrons, mentors and contacts you need to support you in whatever path you choose to take. Individuals and organizations who are in a position to help you and to open doors for you, will somehow find their way into your life. The presence of the celestial Dragon always attracts abundance and success, and this year, inviting in this Dragon brings a very special kind of good fortune indeed.

Invoking the power of THE EIGHT IMMORTALS

Another excellent energizer for the center is the **8 Celestial Immortals Plaque**. The 8 Immortals bring eight kinds of good fortune and protects against harm. In Chinese mythology, they are a revered group of legendary beings each with a unique talent or ability.

Place the 8 Immortals Plaque in the center of the home in 2021.

These eight saints have been depicted in Chinese art since time immemorial as they are believed to bestow wealth, longevity and spiritual awakening on all who glance upon them.

Depicted as a group, they bring a balanced basket of good fortune and protection for the whole family. They hail from the 8 different compass directions and are usually shown with their unique symbols representing the luck each brings.

Zhang Guo Lao, protector of the North, **brings the luck of good descendants**. His symbol is the bamboo flute and his element is Water. He enjoys drinking wine and is famous for making his own which had curative and healing powers. He is said to be able to drink poison without harm and offers protection against the dark arts. He is often shown with his companion, the mule.

Chao Guo Jiu, protector of the Northeast, **brings the luck of control**. He is excellent for those in positions of authority who have to motivate and retain the support of those they command. His element is Earth and his symbol are the castanets. According to legend, he went to great lengths to avoid casualties of war, protecting the innocent from harm during battle. He is skilled in the magical arts and possesses great wisdom and charisma to lead with great authority.

Lee Dong Bin, protector of the West, **brings protection against evil**. His element is Metal and his implement is the Magic Sword. He is famed for being a great scholar and poet, and for his exceptional intelligence. While he had certain character flaws – he was a serial womanizer - he was known for his dedication to helping others elevate their spiritual growth.

He Xian Gu, protector of the Southwest, **bestows family and marriage luck**. Her element is Earth and her symbol is the Lotus Blossom. The only lady among the 8, she has also grown to become a symbol of woman power. She is often accompanied by a mythical bird said to reign over all birds, bringing new opportunities from near and far. She helps stabilize married couples, protecting the sacred sanctity of marriage and bestowing a happy family life. She protects against troublemakers who threaten to break up happy families. For those who are single, she is said to attract marriage opportunities and suitable suitors.

Han Xiang Zi, protector of the Southeast, **brings healing energies** to those who are sick, but more particularly, he helps heal those with a broken heart. His element is Wood and his symbol is the flute. His legendary past involves the tragic love story where he fell in love with the daughter of the Dragon King, who did not grant the couple his blessings. Theirs was a star-crossed romance without a happy ending, but the bamboo flute he wields was said to be a gift from his beloved. Playing on his flute healed him emotionally, and from there on he vowed to help others the same way.

Lan Chai He, protector of the Northwest, **brings scholastic and creative luck**. His element is Metal and his symbol the flower basket. He is often shown with his swan, symbolic of his lyrical gifts. He is said to have become immortal when the Monkey King bestowed 500 years of magic upon him. His companion is the Monkey. As well as his flair for the arts, he is said to possess a sharp intelligence and wit.

Han Zhong Li, protector of the East, **brings longevity and wealth**. His element is Wood and his symbols are the magical fan and peach. His fan is said to have the ability to heal the sick, even bring the dead back to life, as well as turning stones to silver and gold. His peach is the fruit of immortality which grants a long life filled with happiness.

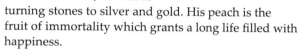

Tie Guai Lee, protector of the South, **brings wisdom and healing**. His element is Fire and his symbol is the Bottle Gourd. He is often depicted as an unkempt old man with disheveled hair, taking on the appearance of a beggar. His chosen role is to care for those who are sick, poor or in need.

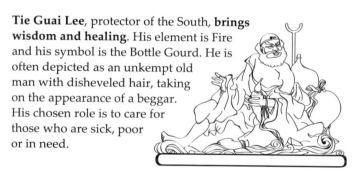

Enhance for Future Prosperity
in the Northeast

The animal sign of the year, the Ox plays host to the *Future Prosperity Star #9*. This star signifies imminent wealth just about to ripen, and the closer we get to Period 9, which starts Feb 4th 2024, the shorter the waiting time for what is considered "future wealth". The #9 is also a magnifying star, which gains power as we head into Period 9. The Ox sign this year thus gets energized with the presence of this star in its sector. The NE is also the place of the Tiger, who features as always in the year's Paht Chee in the month pillar.

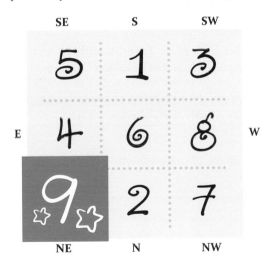

The NE plays host to the "Future Prosperity Star"

The powerful Fire star #9 brings vitality to all who come under its influence, and its presence in the ruling animal sector bodes well for the coming year. This star benefits homes that face NE, and individuals whose bedrooms or office rooms are located NE, as well as those born under the signs of Ox and Tiger.

The #9 in the NE suggests that the central #6 heavenly star gets strengthened. This is a lucky star for most of the year, except for months when monthly flying stars here are unfavourable – i.e. March, May, July, August and December 2021. When unfavourable monthly stars visit, ensure you have the relevant cures in place and keep this sector less active during these times.

ENHANCERS FOR THE NORTHEAST

The NE benefits from the **9 Golden Dragons Plaque** featuring nine celestial Dragons that bestow power and generates the capacity to pursue all one's grandest ambitions conviction and courage.

Having nine Dragons in the NE allows you to stay focused on long-term goals without getting distracted,

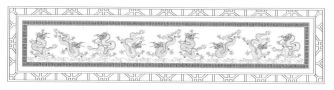

Display the 9 Golden Dragons Plaque in the NE.

or discouraged by short-term difficulties. They protect you against those who wish to see you fail, and shields you from the effects of less ambitious relatives or acquaintances who do not have your vision.

Displaying this plaque in the NE of your home or office ensures you have the support of not one but *nine* Dragons, the number that symbolizes completion and abundance. The number 9 is a magical number as it is a number that always reduces back to itself when multiplied. It also strengthens the #9 star, which is getting stronger as we move rapidly towards a fast-approaching Period of 9.

BUILD YOUR WEALTH: You should also activate the NE with a collection of **Wealth Cabinets**. These wealth cabinets symbolize an accumulation of asset wealth, meaning that the money you make accrues into ever-larger amounts that can last into the many generations. Energizing the NE helps you to make enough money so you do not have to spend everything you earn. It allows you to grow wealthy enough to carve out a secure, comfortable and worry-free future for yourself and your loved ones.

Activate for Love & Romance
in the EAST

The Peach Blossom Star #4 settles into in the East sector this year. This star gets greatly enhanced in 2021 as the East is the place of the Rabbit, the creature associated with the Moon, and with the Goddess of the Moon who governs all fortunes to do with love, romance and relationships. Legend has it that when you catch the attention of the Moon Goddess, she aids you in all matters related to the heart, improving relations between lovers and even matchmaking those who are destined to be together.

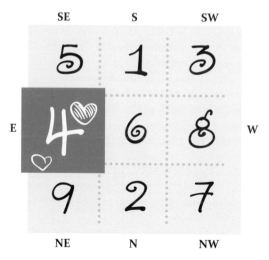

The East plays host to the Peach Blossom Star,
which brings romance.

For those who are single, activating this sector with the **Rabbit in the Moon** awakens the powers of **Moon Goddess**, alerting her to all wishes to do with affairs of the heart. Enhancing this sector promotes the success of relationships, attracts marriage opportunities, smooths interactions between spouses, and imbues stale marriages with a newfound passion and vigour.

> The EAST becomes the place of the MOON RABBIT in 2021, harnessing the power of the Lunar Mansions to bring great love and romance into the lives of those who activate this luck.

This is the sector to enhance if love is what you are looking for! This year we have designed the **Rabbit in the Moon**, the earthly messenger of this lunar goddess. Placing this activator in the East will help singles meet their soulmates and forever partners, while helping those who are already married to  keep their spouses. Remember that this year's Paht Chee generates the unfavourable *External Flower of Romance Star*, which can cause problems within already existing relationships, resulting in unwanted love triangles and other outside disturbances to a love relationship. Invoking the blessings of the **Rabbit in the Moon** ensures that only the positive aspects of love materialize. It will also protect against unpleasantness associated with matters of the heart. They say there is nothing sweeter than love, but they also say that nothing breaks like a heart – remember the song by Mark Ronson and Miley Cyrus? Heartache and heartbreak can be far more painful than physical pain; the #4 in the East brings the Moon Rabbit to life and provides a solution for those looking for happiness in love.

ATTRACTING MARRIAGE OPPORTUNITIES

For those looking for a soul mate, someone you can settle down with and make a future with, or if you are already dating but your partner seems a long way off from proposing marriage, you can speed things along with the help of your **Peach Blossom Animal**. Our new Peach Blossom animals the **Rat**, **Rabbit**, **Horse** and **Rooster** come with trees of fortune enhanced with potent symbols of love and marriage. The **Peach Blossom Rat** brings love and marriage opportunities to the **Rabbit**, **Boar** and **Sheep**. If you are looking for love that leads to marriage, or you would like your current partner to propose, display a **Peach Blossom Rat** in the NORTH, or in the EAST in 2021.

Peach Blossom
Rat

For students,
activate the Scholastic Star in the EAST

For young people and anyone pursuing their studies, engaged in research or in search of new knowledge, they can activate the scholastic star of the year which flies to the East in 2021. The #4 is also the star number that brings study and exam luck; when properly activated, it has the power to help you achieve success in anything related to scholastic accolades. Enhancing this star improves clarity of mind, allowing you to absorb new knowledge and to process it with much greater efficiency. Anything requiring cognitive

The #4 star in the East is also the Star of Scholarship

reasoning and abilities gets enhanced when you harness the energies of this star number.

The #4 Scholastic Star also boosts creativity and original thinking, allowing you to better come up with unique and innovative new ideas. This star gets strengthened this year, as it is a Wood star flying into a Wood sector.

ENHANCE THE SCHOLASTIC STAR: The best way to activate the #4 for scholastic luck is to carry **Manjushri's Gau**. Manjushri is the Buddha of Wisdom, and when you call on his help, he slices through your ignorance so only wisdom remains. His flaming sword removes all that is obscured in your mind, allowing you to think with a clear head so you can map out effective solutions to everything you are pursuing.

For students taking exams, having Manjushri's support enables them to recall everything they have revised and studied, and to write excellent answers in their exam. Manjushri boosts everything to do with wisdom and intelligence,

and helps one to make wise choices. He
ensures one constantly sees the big
picture, while also filling in the details.
For school-going children, they can
clip **Manjushri's "Dhih" Scholastic
Amulet** onto their schoolbag. This
specially-designed amulet sums
up all of Manjushri's wisdom and
blessings, providing an endless
stream of support, reinforcement and
inspiration.

FOR EXAM LUCK:

For students taking important exams and hoping
to do well, there is no better enhancer than the
Dragon Carp. The carp that jumps over the
Dragon Gate and successfully transforms into a
Dragon is the best symbol for anyone aspiring
to scholastic success. It promotes the luck of
scholarship and helps students excel in all their
exams. The Dragon Carp also generates a strong
sense of self-motivation, ensuring one does not
fall into bad company or get side-tracked into
unproductive tasks. This is the best enhancer
for children or teenagers looking to perform
well in important exams, to win awards, to gain
scholarships and grants and to gain admission
into colleges of their choice.

The academic path of today is filled with potholes and pitfalls, far more than in the old days, as everything has become more competitive. More and more people are fighting for fewer places at the top universities; at school, children are faced with competition from classmates with Tiger parents in the sidelines egging them on. For a young mind, it can all become too much, and with all the expectations heaped on young shoulders these days, sometimes all it takes is one bad test or one bad result to cause a child to throw in the towel and just give up.

As parents, we need to imbue in our children not just the impetus to keep striving for the top, but help them understand there will be bumps and disappointments along the way. It is not necessary to perform every single day of the year, to come out top in every single test; what is important is to peak when it counts and to perform when it matters. The **Dragon Carp** stabilizes one's mind, helping a child along the academic path and to navigate all that comes his or her way with a strong and mature mind, resulting in success when it truly matters.

Transform Five Yellow Misfortune Star
in the Southeast

The bogus star, the Five Yellow, makes its way into the Southeast this year. The good news is that because the Southeast is a Wood Sector, it mitigates the extent of damage of this dangerous Earth star, as Wood destroys Earth in the cycle of elements. When the Five Yellow flies into a Wood sector, misfortune can be turned into opportunity. This is why we have designed this year's **Five Element Pagoda with a Tree of Life**. This alters the effects of the *wu wang*, suppressing the darker side of this star while

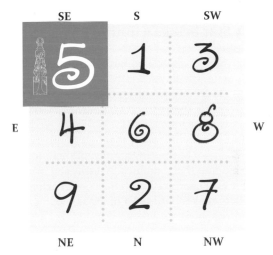

SE	S	SW
5	1	3
4	6	8
9	2	7
NE	N	NW

The 5 Yellow afflicts the SE in 2021 but with the correct cure, this Five Yellow has the potential to bring great good luck!

harnessing its benevolent powers. This star affects those living in homes that face SE, those with bedrooms or work rooms in the SE, and those born in years of the Dragon and Snake.

If your house has more than one level, make sure you have a **Five Element Pagoda with Tree of Life** on every floor. Keep the SE of the home free from too much activity and noise and avoid renovations in this part of the home in 2021.Whatever you do, DO NOT renovate the SE of the home this year.

Victory Star brings winning luck
to the South

The White Star #1 associated with victory and winning luck makes its way to the South this year. This star allows you to triumph in any situation and to attain success over any competition you may face. In 2021, this star benefits those whose bedrooms are located South, and all those living in homes that face South. Anyone who spends a lot of time in this part of their home can also tap into the good luck that this star brings by keeping it well energized with the correct activators. The livelier you keep this part of the home, the better!

The Victory Star this year is made more potent as it is supported by not one but **TWO Big Auspicious Stars** from the 24 Mountains, as well as the **Golden Deity**

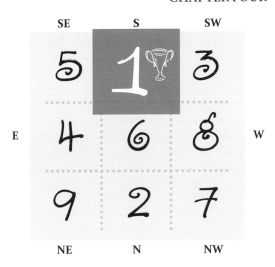

The South sector enjoys the Victory Star in 2021.

Star, echoing the benefits of the ruling star of the year, the #6 Heaven Star. All this serves to increase the power and effectiveness of this star, so it is really worthwhile to actively enhance this star this year. Because the South is the sector governing the reputation of the household, the #1 here also improves one's standing and repute in various circles – work, social, etc.

ACTIVATE THE VICTORY STAR:
The best enhancer for the Victory Star is the
Victorious Windhorse Carrying a Jewel. The
Windhorse is the very essence of success luck,
known as the magical steed of the folk hero
King Gesar, who when riding his Windhorse
could never be defeated. His horse with flaming
red coat has become synonymous with success
and victory, and his image is what is needed
whenever one needs to boost one's chances
against others in any kind of competitive
situation. In 2021, we recommend that everyone
displays the Victorious Windhorse in the South.
This sector is also the home sector of the Horse,
an auspicious creature that emanates pure Fire
energy. Displaying images and figurines of
horses in the South is thus very appropriate and
auspicious indeed.

Activate the
#1 Star in the
South with
the Victorious
Windhorse.

BOOST POWER AND AUTHORITY:
For those in positions of leadership and management, the best way to enhance your effectiveness as a leader is with the help of the **Ru Yi**. The Ru Yi is the royal scepter of power, which bestows "the right to rule". In ancient China, anyone in any kind of power would never be seen without a Ru Yi at his side. You can place your Ru Yi in front of you on your work desk, or carry in your bag.

The **Crimson Red Ru Yi with Bats** brings the luck of **success and abundance**. Any boss, head or leader can use the help of this Ru Yi to ensure things between all in their group stay harmonious, joyful and productive at all times. It attracts the luck of abundance and success, so whatever is pursued turns out fruitful and effective. It helps you to ensure all your final goals are reached in the most harmonious way.

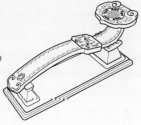

Anyone in any kind of leadership position needs a Ru Yi.

The **Deep Blue Ru Yi with 8 Auspicious Symbols** brings the luck of **wealth**. This Ru Yi includes the Victory Banner for winning luck, the Double Fish for abundance, the Parasol for protection, the Conch for good news, the Wheel for sustainability, the Mystic Knot for longevity, the Vase for completion and the Lotus for good intentions.

These symbols of good fortune are the magical implements of the Eight Immortals, and act as vessels of their power. Carrying images of their magical symbols on a Ru Yi imbues you with a complete collection of the different kinds of luck you need to reach your full potential as a leader.

The **Yellow Ru Yi with Celestial Dragon** brings the luck of **power and position**. Those operating in political environments or in politics need this Ru Yi! It bestows charisma and magnetism, and endows strength to make your position one that is stable and secure. It ensures you do not get plotted against and overthrown. It protects against betrayal and treachery and gives you power over those on the outside as well as on the inside.

The SOUTH is the place to activate if success, victory, fame and reputation is what you seek.

Suppress the Quarrelsome Star
in the Southwest

The Quarrelsome Star #3 flies to the Southwest, bringing hostile energy and complications associated with arguments, misunderstandings and court cases. The #3 star can also cause serious aggravations that lead to violence and tragedy. This affliction affects anyone with a bedroom in the SW, those whose main doors face SW, and those born in years of the Sheep and Monkey. It also affects the Matriarch of the household. The #3 star is especially strong this year,

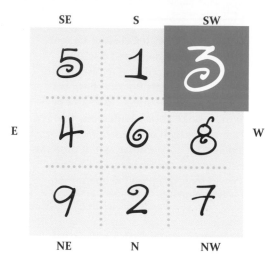

Beware the #3 quarrelsome star in the SW this year.

as the intrinsic Wood energy of the star dominates the Earth energy of the SW. The effects of this star are made worse as the SW also plays host to the **Yin House** from the 24 Mountains. All this suggests that this affliction MUST be taken seriously.

Anything that suggests Fire is an effective cure, so keeping the lights turned on brightly in this sector will help combat the negative energies of this star. **The colour red** is also suitable, so red curtains, rugs and cushion covers here will help very much indeed.

CURES FOR THE QUARRELSOME STAR:
For 2021, the best remedy for the Quarrelsome Star in the SW is the **Nine Phoenix Plaque** in red and gold. These celestial birds in red and gold - which represent the elements of Fire and Metal - work to subdue this troublesome Wood Star. The Fire energy engulfs the Wood of the #3, while the Metal energy of the gold effectively subdues it.

The Nine Phoenix Plaque is an excellent cure against the #3 Quarrelsome Star.

We also recommend placing **red carpets** in this sector, or in the SW portion of any room you spend a lot of time in. Another effective cure for the #3 are the **Red Peace and Harmony Apples**. In Chinese, the word for peaceful is *Ping*, which sounds like the word for apple – *Ping Kor*. This year's Peace Apples come embossed with the English word "Peace" and the Chinese rhyming couplet carrying the meaning "If your intentions are good and your heart is pure, the world will be peaceful."

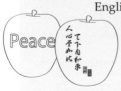

Place this pair of apples in the SW to ensure all members of the household stay supportive of one another, and to prevent clashes and conflict from arising. Also an excellent cure for use within the office to maintain a productive and supportive environment between colleagues and workmates.

Enhance Prosperity Star 8
in the West

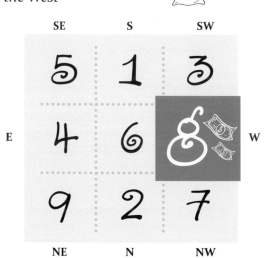

The Wealth Star #8 flies to the West this year.

The very lucky Wealth Star #8 makes its way to the West, the sector of the Rooster. This star is also known as the *Current Prosperity Star*, as we are currently in the Period of 8. The West is the sector that represents children and descendants, suggesting that the wealth that this sector brings will last into the long term, reaching future generations and for many generations to come. It points to a successful accumulation of assets over time if properly energized.

In 2021, the West can be considered one of the luckiest areas of the home, because it enjoys this auspicious #8 star. The strong energy of the current period emanating from this sector benefits all homes whose main entrances face West, and all bedrooms and offices located in the West benefit from this luck. The West is also the place of the youngest daughter, so the wealth this sector brings benefits the young girls of the house.

WEALTH luck takes root in the WEST sector this year so this is the area of the home you should enhance for greater prosperity luck.

Remember that to activate the luck of this auspicious star #8, the West should be thoroughly imbued with yang energy - this means lots of activity, lots of noise and plenty of bright lights. When there is movement, sound, chatter and merry-making, the number 8 comes to life, bringing good fortune and big prosperity. In the constellations, 8 is a "man-made star" with two assistants – on the right and on the left - so that at its strongest moments, it brings wealth and great nobility.

When the 8 can turn dangerous...
Beware however. The number becomes negative when afflicted by structures in the environment that threaten its location. If the West sector of your home has too much Metal energy, or if there are harmful physical structures that cause poison arrows to direct threatening energy your way, that is when the number 8 can bring harm to young children especially young daughters of the household, causing illness to arise. If there are such structures external to your home,

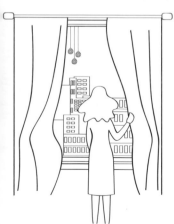

but towards the West, it is important to block the view with curtains, or dissipate the killing energy with **facetted crystal balls**. These will disperse the worst of the killing breath before it has the chance to enter your home.

If the view from your window to the WEST is of a threatening looking building with sharp edges or poison arrows, keep the curtains in this area closed to block the offending view from spoiling your feng shui. Hang facetted crystal balls here.

ACTIVATE FOR WEALTH IN THE WEST
The best way to manifest wealth luck in 2021 is the make sure the West part of your home is well-energized with wealth symbols. Because this is the year of the Ox, this creature is especially lucky as it symbolizes harnessing the good fortune of the year. Because the West represents children and descendants, this prosperity luck benefits the whole family not just in the present but into the long term.

The image of the Ox has great power to attract abundant good fortune in 2021. Displaying images of the Ox in all sizes and permutations is so lucky this year! For the collectors among you, a good time to start "collecting" Ox images.

A fabulous wealth enhancer for this year is the **Asset Wealth Bull**. This Bull holds the symbolic and subliminal message "May the market bull for you"! With resplendent red saddle and surrounded by coins, ingots and symbols of prosperity, this bull energizes for wealth of the kind that can accumulate into expanded net worth, the kind that provides meaningful disposable income, providing a worry-free future.

Display the Asset Wealth Bull for wealth that grows and expands your net worth!

To tap the hidden wealth of the year, display the **Ox finding Hidden Wealth**. This Ox is depicted calmly and unobtrusively grazing in a field full of coins, sniffing out hidden wealth and opportunities. In a year with little obvious wealth but a lot of hidden wealth, this Ox generates the luck that allows you to tap the full potential of the year.

Invite in the "Ox Finding Hidden Wealth" to tap the full potential of the year.

Another great activator for this year's wealth star is the **Tree Bringing 3 Kinds of Wealth**.

Trees always depict growth energy, and when they look like money trees, they really do bring the luck of wealth into the home! Our tree this year has been designed to represent the manifestation of 3 different kinds of wealth - Asset Wealth, Income Wealth and Growth Wealth. Having all three kinds of wealth brings you not just enough to lead a comfortable life now, it gives you security and peace of mind and allows you to plan for the future. This year's wealth tree also features 12 lucky charms to signify abundance in all forms entering your life - the Double Fish, the Apple, the Treasure Chest, the Golden Ingot, the Wealth Vase, the Abacus, the I-Ching Coin, Gold bars, the 4-leafed clover the Maneki Neko Lucky Cat and the Pot of Gold.

This year's wealth tree represents not just prosperity luck but also the luck of asset accumulation. This symbolises your wealth growing and your net worth expanding.

Beware Betrayal & Loss Star
in the Northwest

A dangerous aspect of this year's chart is the #7 Robbery Star in the NW. This brings loss and betrayal energies to the Patriarch, which not only means the patriarch of the family, but leaders, bosses, managers and anyone responsible for the welfare or livelihood of others. The presence of the #7 in the NW suggests that the Patriarch could get cheated, conned or betrayed. It brings the energy that suggests you should keep your friends close but your enemies closer.

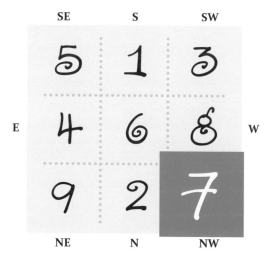

The NW, the sector of the Patriarch and Leader, gets afflicted by the #7 Loss and Betrayal Star in 2021.

In 2021, keep your friends close but your enemies closer!

Stay alert like a hawk, as treachery can strike at any moment. The energies of the year could corrupt even the most trustworthy of friends and the most loyal of employees. The #7 Robbery Star, like its namesake, describes a situation when you are cheated out of money; but it can also manifest as an actual robbery. We recommend all who stay out late, or who venture anywhere even remotely unsafe, to carry the **Nightspot Protection Amulet**. Because this star affects the NW, it harms the Father the most, but there can be knock-on adverse effects on the rest of the family, or the rest of a leader's charges.

CURE FOR #7 STAR: This year the best cure for the #7 star in the home is the **Anti-Burglary Plaque with Door Guardians**. These Door Gods with spear in the ready are depicted with the Anti-Burglary Amulets, with the Chinese proverb, "May your family be blessed with peace, safety and abundant joy, may your home be filled with everlasting happiness."

Display in the NW to ensure your home stays protected against unexpected and unwanted intruders, who may cause not just loss of property and possessions, but loss of peace of mind. These door guardians will help keep your family protected through the year.

BEWARE BETRAYAL:

This year, risk of betrayal is rife as the #7 star occupies the NW, the location of the leader. Betrayal means duplicity from those you trust, those you least suspect and therefore those you are most vulnerable to. While it feels nasty to get cheated by conmen and people you do not know, when betrayals come from those closest to you, the harm is emotional as well as physical. The loss is no longer merely monetary, it hits a nerve deep within that can be difficult to take and recover from. This year, because opportunity for this to happen gets increased, we suggest to remove temptation where you can, watch your back, and carry symbols to protect against this kind of bad luck. Carry the **Kuan Kung Anti-Betrayal Amulet**. This specially-designed talisman features the amulet that protects against being stabbed in the back, with the mantra that ensures the protection is effective.

Kuan Kung Anti-
Betrayal Amulet

PROTECT AGAINST BEING CHEATED:
For those engaging in high-risk deals carry
the **Anti-Cheating Amulet** to ensure you do
not get conned by unscrupulous people. An
excellent amulet for business people and for
anyone dealing with new acquaintances who
maybe be untrustworthy.

PROTECTION AGAINST THE DARK ARTS:
Another form of harm can come from those who
practice black magic. Especially in the East, such arts
are more common than you think. Even if you do not
subscribe or "believe" in this kind of power, it exists.
Someone who projects negative thoughts against you,
whether out of spite, jealousy or some other reason,
does not even have to be skilled in these methods to
send negative hexes and projectiles your way!

For example, if someone curses you on the street
because they are angry at the way you drive, this
can result in the same kind of misfortune effect as
someone actively plotting or using black magic against
you. The latter is of course more serious, but whenever
one is weak in terms of spirit essence and element
luck, they can succumb badly when someone forms
negative thoughts and sends those thoughts their way.

The best protection against this kind of harm is the **28
Hums Protection Wheel**, which features the powerful

Heart Sutra on the back. These sacred syllables together with this powerful sutra ensures that whatever projectiles are sent your way cannot reach you. A vital cure for anyone with enemies, who are engaged in high stakes deals, or anyone who may have offended someone intentionally or unintentionally.

28 Hums
Protection Wheel

Suppress Illness Star
in the North

The #2 Illness Star flies to the North, and because North is of the Water element, it cannot do anything on its own to weaken the energies of the #2, an Earth star. The Illness Star is further strengthened as it is supported by the **Yin House Star** in North 2, the sector of the Rat. This boosts the potency of this star, making the North sector dangerous for those who are elderly, frail or prone to illness.

It is important for anyone whose bedroom is facing North, or whose home faces North to suppress the Illness Star with strong cures.

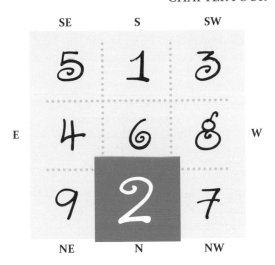

SE	S	SW
5	1	3
E 4	6	8 W
9	**2**	7
NE	N	NW

The North gets afflicted by the Illness Star this year.

CURE FOR THE ILLNESS STAR:
In 2021, a good cure for the Illness Star is the **Healing Deer Carrying Vase of Longevity with Linzhi**. The deer is renowned by the Chinese for their powerful curative properties and is often seen as the companion of the God of Longevity, Sau Seng Kong. With the world caught up in fears of epidemics and pandemics where there seems no escape with a proper cure a long time coming, the

Healing Deer

deer is an excellent shield against this kind of illness. Display in the North of the home this year. The Healing Deer is an excellent symbol of good health in the year 2021.

Another potent cure against the Illness Star #2 is the **Medicine Buddha and the 7 Sugatas Gau**. Medicine Buddha always comes to the aid of those who are suffering when one calls for his help. His area of expertise is in the removal of poisons, disease and illness, and the **Medicine Buddha and the 7 Sugatas Gau** features all 8 of his emanations, and his powerful mantras in whole. You  can place in the North of the home to stay under his protection constantly. Excellent for anyone who is ill or feeling unwell.

You can also chant his mantra daily:
**TADYATHA OM BHEKHANDZYE
BHEKHANDZYE MAHA BHEKHANDZYE
(BHEKHANDZYE) RADZA SAMUGATE SOHA**

For those suffering from a chronic ailment, we suggest that you get yourself a dedicated **Medicine Buddha Mala** to chant with. The more you chant his mantra over the mala, the more powerful the mala will become. Keep the mala with you always, and whenever you have spare time, bring it out and chant. You can also wear the mala as an accessory around your wrist or neck.

HEART MANTRA
OF ARYA VAIROCHANA

WOFS™

AGAINST COVID-19:
To protect against the coronavirus specifically, the best cure is to invite in an image of the **Buddha Vairocana**, who brings blessings of good health but also provides strong protection against contagious diseases. Display his image as a figurine, and also carry his image in the form of a **Gold Talisman Card** which we have made available to help tide us through these challenging times.

AFFLICTIONS OF 2021
TAI SUI *in the NORTHEAST*

The TAI SUI or God of the Year always occupies the sector of the ruling animal sign of the year. This year, he occupies the palace of the Ox, Northeast 1. The Tai Sui is the celestial force that governs all that happens on Earth, and when one has his support and blessings, very little can go wrong, but when one offends him, his wrath knows no bounds.

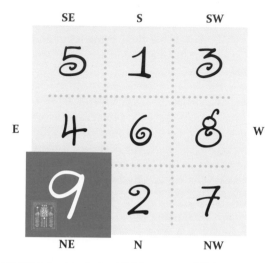

	SE	**S**	**SW**
	5	1	3
E	4	6	8	**W**
	9	2	7
	NE	**N**	**NW**

The Tai Sui resides in the NE this year, and it is important to keep him on your side. Place the Tai Sui Plaque 2021 here.

It is a matter of course and tradition for most Chinese who believe, to offer prayers to Tai Sui at the start of the year, humbly asking for his help and support for the coming year. In feng shui, the creature that is known to appease him is the celestial chimera the **Dragon Pi Xie**, so we always recommend to place this in the location of the Tai Sui.

The Dragon Pi Xie is said to appease the Tai Sui. Place in the NE in 2021.

PROTECTION: What is even more important is to place the **Tai Sui Plaque** with his image and invocation as a sign of respect. In 2021, place this in the NE1 sector. Animal signs especially affected by the Tai Sui this year are the

Earth signs of Sheep, Dragon and Dog, while the Ox whose location he occupies should also be mindful of his presence there. For these 4 signs, we also recommend carrying the **Tai Sui Amulet** at all times throughout the year.

THREE KILLINGS in the EAST

This affliction is said to bring three types of misfortune – loss of wealth, loss of reputation and loss of a loved one. All three are devastating, and when not one but three forms of bad luck hit you at once, the loss can be difficult and extremely distressing. This is another affliction that is important to take note of and to cure.

Firstly, NEVER have your back to the Three Killings affliction, so in 2021, DO NOT SIT FACING WEST,

EVEN if WEST is your best direction! Do not sit with your back to the East, as the Three Killings is the kind of affliction that stabs you in the back, when you are least suspecting. It carries the characteristic of hitting you when you are most comfortable and least aware. When things are at their calmest, beware, because the storm is about to pound and crash down...

NEVER HAVE YOUR BACK TO THE EAST this year! Make sure you do not get stabbed by the dangerous 3 Killings affliction!

CURE FOR THE THREE KILLINGS: Place the **3 Celestial Shields** to combat the Three Killings.

These shields act as effective armour sheltering you from the effects of this difficult affliction. All homes should display these shields in the EAST in 2021. Anyone with something to lose, who operate where stakes are high, or who are going through years of low element luck are also recommended to carry the **3 Celestial Shields Amulet** when on the go. Use as a keychain or bag decoration.

Compatibilities with other Signs in 2021

Chapter 5

Rabbit's stakes in the love game gets a big boost this year

The Rabbit emerges in 2021 much stronger and far more optimistic, and its stakes in the love game improves big time! Your popularity with friends and relatives gets a big boost, a great relief from last year when you were afflicted by the troublesome Five Yellow. Your social life generates much joy, bringing you love and inspiration. You may find yourself rekindling old friendships, mending relationships that went a bit wobbly last year, and everyone you meet acts more kindly towards you. Those looking for love should open your heart and accept all the loving vibes coming your way!

Many different influences come into play each year to determine how one animal sign gets along with another. Chinese astrology has so many permutations that it is difficult to take note of everything, but examining some of the main variables can give useful insights to the general mood and compatibility between any two signs in any year. The annual energies of the year have a larger bearing on the effect on your relationships than you may be aware of, and understanding these effects allows you to be more effective in all your interactions.

When you find the keys to unlock what makes your connections tick, not only will this help with your happiness levels, it also improves your productivity and success potential.

Every animal sign under the Chinese Zodiac system has certain signs they are naturally drawn towards; certain signs make better spouses, others make more exciting lovers, others still work better when you remain platonic friends. Certain pairings thrive in a business relationship, as boss and employee, mentor and mentee; others work well as parent and child, siblings, sporting teammates or drinking buddies; while others still, have the potential to change your life in a big way.

There are also certain signs you need to stay alert to and be wary of. One's Zodiac Adversary is the animal sign born six years apart from you, the sign directly opposite you in the Zodiac wheel – but in certain years, your "natural enemy" can become a useful ally, while in others, you would be best advised to stay well clear of each other. Having knowledge of how the year's energies influence your relationships will give you the edge when it comes to how you relate to others in any given year.

In this section, we analyse the relationship between the Rabbit and the other signs in the Zodiac, looking in particular at the quality and nature of the relationships as determined by the influences of 2021.

1. Alliance of Allies

There are four affinity groupings that form natural allies in the horoscope. The three signs in each group have similar thought processes, aspirations and goals. Their attitudes are alike, and their support of each other is immediate and instinctive. If there is an alliance within a family unit amongst siblings, or between spouses and their child, the family is incredibly supportive, giving strength to each other. In good years, auspicious luck gets multiplied.

Astrological allies always get along. Any falling out is temporary. They trust each other and close ranks against external threats. Good astrological feng shui comes from carrying the image of your allies, especially when they are going through good years.

When all three signs in a particular year has good fortune, the alliance is strengthened. But in years when one sign stands out with superior luck, the others in its grouping can "lean" on that sign to lift itself up. The Rabbit belongs to the grouping of Diplomats in the Zodiac, comprising the Rabbit, Sheep and Boar.

This year, the strongest link in the Rabbit's alliance of allies is you, the Rabbit. But all three signs enjoy decent luck this year.

For the Rabbit, any relationship with either Sheep or Boar brings you great good fortune. When the Rabbit gets involved with a Sheep or Boar, there is a very natural familiarity that nurtures a deep and lasting devotion. Together, you enjoy a blissful kind of contentment. You value peace and harmony above

ALLY GROUPINGS	ANIMALS	CHARACTERISTICS
Competitors	Rat, Dragon, Monkey	Competent, Tough, Resolute
Intellectuals	Ox, Snake, Rooster	Generous, Focused, Resilient
Enthusiasts	Dog, Tiger, Horse	Aggressive, Rebellious, Coy
Diplomats	Boar, Sheep, Rabbit	Creative, Kind, Emotional

all other signs of the Zodiac, so whatever differences you have can be resolved amicably with willing compromise from all parties. When a Rabbit is paired with a Sheep or Boar, you have great potential to make it to the golden years.

If you do not have close friends or alliances born in years of the Sheep or Boar, you benefit from displaying images or figurines of the Sheep and Boar in your home. Hang beautiful and inspiring art of these animals in your home. You can also carry images of your astrological allies as talismans to bring greater love and friendship luck into your life.

For the Rabbit, displaying images of Sheep or Boar in your living space brings you the luck of friendship.

2. Zodiac Soulmates

Another natural ally for you is your Zodiac soulmate. In Chinese astrology, there are six pairs of signs that create six Zodiac Houses of yin and yang soulmates. Each pair creates powerful bonding on a cosmic level. Marriages or business unions between people belonging to the same Zodiac House are extremely auspicious. In a marriage, there is great love and devotion, and in a commercial partnership, it promises much wealth and success. Such a pairing is also good between professional colleagues or between siblings.

The strength of each pair is different, each having a defining strength with some making better commercial than marriage partners. How successful you are as a pair depends on how you bond. The table on the following page summarizes the key strength of each Zodiac house.

For the Rabbit, your Zodiac Soulmate is the Tiger. Together you form the *House of Growth and Development*, with both bringing their formidable talents into the mix. The Tiger uses strength while the Rabbit uses negotiation. The Tiger provides the courage, the Rabbit the strategy. When these two come together, you never quarrel over the details or over who gets to do what, because you understand each other's unique strengths and assets. You bring out the best in each other, and are as happy whether your relationship is a personal or professional one.

HOUSES OF PAIRED SOULMATES

ANIMALS	YIN/YANG	ZODIAC HOUSE	TARGET UNLEASHED
Rat & Ox	YANG /YIN	*House of Creativity & Cleverness*	The Rat initiates The Ox completes
Tiger & Rabbit	YANG /YIN	*House of Growth & Development*	The Tiger uses strength The Rabbit uses negotiation
Dragon & Snake	YANG /YIN	*House of Magic & Spirituality*	The Dragon takes action The Snake creates magic
Horse & Sheep	YANG /YIN	*House of Passion & Sexuality*	The Horse embodies strength & courage The Sheep embodies seduction & allure
Monkey & Rooster	YANG /YIN	*House of Career & Commerce*	The Monkey creates good strategy The Rooster takes timely action
Dog & Boar	YANG /YIN	*House of Domesticity*	The Dog creates alliances The Boar benefits

3. Secret Friends

Another extremely powerful affinity arises when two secret friends come together. There are six pairs of secret friends in the Zodiac. Love, respect and goodwill flow freely between you. Once forged, your bond is extremely hard to break. Even when you yourselves want to break it, it will be hard for either party to walk away. This pair of signs will stick together through thick and thin. For the Rabbit, your secret friend is the Dog. This is a very synergistic coupling as there is a mutual adoration and easy comradeship that springs forth spontaneously when you are together. Very few pairings in the Zodiac get as cosy as the Dog and the Rabbit.

PAIRINGS OF SECRET FRIENDS			
🐁	Rat	Ox	🐂
🐗	Boar	Tiger	🐅
🐕	Dog	Rabbit	🐇
🐉	Dragon	Rooster	🐓
🐍	Snake	Monkey	🐒
🐎	Horse	Sheep	🐑

These are two signs who are not only passionate as lovers, they are best friends as well. When you get together with the Dog sign, there is real chance of long term happiness, and even when difficulties crop up, you both emerge even stronger. The Rabbit and Dog enjoy a of karmic affinity that is unrivalled!

4. Peach Blossom Links

Each alliance of allies has a special relationship with one of the four primary signs of Horse, Rat, Rooster and Rabbit in that these are the symbolic representations of love and romance for one alliance group of animal signs. These are referred to as Peach Blossom Animals, and the presence of their images in the homes of the matching alliance of allies brings peach blossom luck, which is associated with love and romance.

> The Rabbit belongs to the alliance of Rabbit, Sheep and Boar, which has the Rat as their Peach Blossom link.

The Rabbit benefits from displaying images of the **Peach Blossom Rat** in the home which brings love and marriage opportunities into your life. Place in the North of your home for romance luck.

For the Rabbit, the Rat is your Peach Blossom animal, and displaying images of the Rat in the home brings love and marriage luck to the Rabbit.

5. Seasonal Trinities

Another grouping of signs creates the seasonal trinity combinations that bring the luck of *seasonal abundance*. To many experts, this is regarded as one of the more powerful combinations. When it exists within a family made up of either parent or both parents with one or more children, it indicates that as a family unit, their collective luck can transform all that is negative into positive outcomes. When annual indications of the year are not favourable, the existence of a seasonal combination of signs in any living abode can transform bad luck into better luck, especially during the season indicated by the combination.

Seasonal Trinities of the Horoscope

ANIMAL SIGNS	SEASON	ELEMEMT	DIRECTION
Dragon, Rabbit, Tiger	*Spring*	Wood	East
Snake, Horse, Sheep	*Summer*	Fire	South
Monkey, Rooster, Dog	*Autumn*	Metal	West
Ox, Rat, Boar	*Winter*	Water	North

It is necessary for all three signs to live together or be in the same office working in close proximity for this powerful pattern to work. For greater impact, it is better if they are all using the direction associated with the relevant season. The Rabbit belongs to the Spring Season, its direction is East, and its seasonal group comprises the Tiger, Rabbit and Dragon.

PAIRINGS OF ASTROLOGICAL ENEMIES

🐀	Rat	⟷	Horse	🐎
🐖	Boar	⟷	Snake	🐍
🐕	Dog	⟷	Dragon	🐉
🐇	Rabbit	⟷	Rooster	🐓
🐅	Tiger	⟷	Monkey	🐒
🐂	Ox	⟷	Sheep	🐐

6. Astrological Enemies

Your astrological enemy is the sign that directly confronts yours in the astrology wheel. For the Rabbit, your astrological enemy is the Rooster. Note that your enemy does not necessarily harm you; it only means someone of this sign can never be of any real help to you. There is a six year gap between natural enemies. A marriage between astroligical enemies is not usually recommended. Thus marriage between a Rabbit and Rooster is unlikely to bring lasting happiness unless other indications suggest otherwise. The Rabbit is advised to refrain from getting involved with anyone born in the year of the Rooster, although on a year-by-year basis, this can sometimes be overcome by the annual energies. As a business partnership, this pairing is likely to lead to problems, and in the event of a split, the separation is often acrimonious and painful. Even if passion flows between you at the early stages of your relationship, you are not likely to be happy together in the long run. Rabbit and Rooster are better off pairing up with other signs who are more compatible with them.

If a Rabbit is already married to a Rooster, the solution to improve your prospects for lasting happiness is to introduce the Cardinal Cross into your living space. Display all four animals belonging to the cardinal signs, or display the **Cardinal Cross mirror**, to transform your relationship from one of animosity into one of mutual success together.

For the Rabbit in a relationship with a Rooster, displaying the Cardinal Cross comprising Rat, Rabbit, Horse and Rooster in your shared living space will improve your cosmic connection with one another.

RABBIT with RAT

No natural affinity but better in 2021

These two signs have no natural affinity, but 2021 sees this improve with the energies of the year. Rabbit is feeling amorous and its natural charm may well hook in the unsuspecting Rat. If Rabbit makes the first move, Rat may well fall head over heels for the demure Rabbit. When Rabbit is on a mission, it is very attractive, and with the *Peach Blossom Star* firmly on its side, there is little anyone can do to resist!

In 2021, Rabbit's romance star lures in the Rat. But while the two may enjoy a beautiful year-long romance, chances of things lasting beyond the year are slim.

A blissful time for young lovers looking to pair up for some fun, but when things start getting serious, you may want to think again. Unless your life goals align and you have something substantial in common, a Rat and Rabbit pair may not stand the test of time. You are both sensible personalities, and if already married, by hook or by crook you will make things work, if only for the sake of the children. There is however danger of infidelities. Because you are not natural soulmates, it is easy for either

Enhancing Relationships Amulet

to be taken in by temptation outside the marriage. Best to carry the **Enhancing Relationships Amulet** if you feel something is amiss.

As workmates, the pairing works better this year if Rabbit is in charge. The energies favour Rabbit over Rat, so if Rat is happy to play second fiddle, both benefit. If Rat is the boss, Rabbit will not submit so willingly, and then the problems begin. Rabbit will view Rat's grand schemes with disdain, while Rat's insecurities get increasingly magnified. Rabbit's superciliousness meanwhile will grate on the Rat.

If Rat and Rabbit have no choice but to work together, keep discussions short. Analysis-paralysis could make things heat up and then arguments ensue. A Rat working with a Rabbit needs to pander to Rabbit's natural arrogance, while a Rabbit working with a Rat needs to ensure it does not take and take.

Too long together and the Wood of the Rabbit will start to exhaust the Water of the Rat. Because it will not be an even relationship on any level, the only way this relationship will work is if one is the minor. As parent and child, or teacher and student, as long as there is ample respect, both can be good for the other. But when these two come together as equals, the relationship will not be so easy.

RABBIT with OX

Sharing a Ho Tu connection in 2021

Rabbit and Ox may not look like they have much in common, but when these two signs come together, it is a textbook case of opposites attracting. Rabbit brings out all that is tender in the Ox, and Ox boosts Rabbit's confidence no end.

> These two make a passionate couple. While to the outside both may be serious and motivated types, when together, they melt right into each other's arms.

Rabbit feels safe in an Ox's strong embrace, while Ox comes alive with Rabbit's spirited ideals. While the Ox is generally steady, composed and even stiff with outsiders, with a Rabbit by it side, Ox learns to live life full of joy and delight. Making money and gaining power will always be at the back of the mind of the Ox, but it becomes secondary to the happiness it enjoys in the arms of a Rabbit.

Passion flows freely between these two, and in 2021, this is even more so. The energies of the year work strongly in their favour, with Ox's magnification star joining with Rabbit's wisdom star to find workable solutions to whatever dilemmas they may face. And with their luck, these will happily be few and far between.

In a work situation, it will be Ox calling the shots, but Rabbit is happy to follow. In a partnership, whoever fronts the pairing will work, because neither will clamour for the limelight. Each are happy to allow the other to shine, and this becomes truly a partnership of equals.

> In a marriage, they can build a happy and comfortable life together where money is rarely an issue. Whether they are rich or poor, they find ways to keep each other entertained. They laugh at each other's jokes, and both are secure in their own company and in the company of others

While both Rabbit and Ox have the potential to stray from a marriage, if together, they rarely need to do so, as their appetite for intimacy and romance are on par. They give each other the space each needs, while always being there for one another. They are as happy when together as when they are apart, as each will be only a phonecall away.

This is one of the more fabulous of pairings of the Zodiac, and well worth making the effort for.

RABBIT with TIGER

Bringing each other a lot of luck in 2021

Rabbit and Tiger are both Wood element signs who bring each other a big dose of good fortune luck in 2021. Their flying star numbers combine to create the magical *Ho Tu* connection that injects the union with success, empathy and triumph.

> When Rabbit and Tiger meet, all kinds of positive thoughts fill their minds. They maybe poles apart in terms of personality, but they are a wonderful case of opposites attracting, especially in the coming year.

Rabbit and Tiger in 2021 make an ideal pairing of courage and circumspection. On the surface, these two make unlikely friends or business partners, because Tiger is perceived to be so loud and demanding while Rabbit is so docile and gentle. But in 2021, their contrasting personalities create the perfect balance of courage and contingency, boldness and restraint. And the *Peach Blossom Star* in the Rabbit's corner helps love to blossom beautifully between these two.

Rabbit and Tiger have something very significant in common and can end up even soulmates. Scratch beneath the surface of the Tiger and you discover a completely different personality, someone with the vision to build, create and develop ideas meaningfully. This finds resonance with the Rabbit's secret ambition of wanting to do something meaningful in life.

These two signs enjoy one of best kinds of bonding between two people, allowing them to enjoy a long-lived union and bringing out all that is good in each of them.

As a partnership, they complement each other although their modus operandi may be different. Rabbit will play the diplomat and Tiger will take on the difficult tasks. They aid each other in any plan they carry out together, and they are able to transform their individual natures into a powerful and cohesive partnership. In love, they are blessed by the loving energy of the *Peach Blossom*. Tiger succumbs to Rabbit's affable and calming influence, while Rabbit soaks up Tiger's bright charisma. The significant thing about this union is that both have luck indications that work to bring them together this year, and because these two Wood signs have enough in common, their union can stand the test of time.

FENG SHUI ENHANCER: A Rabbit and Tiger pair in business together can capture substantial commercial success this year. Both should carry or display the **Ho Tu Enhancer** with Dragon Horse.

RABBIT with RABBIT

All loved up in 2021

Two Rabbits make a sweet pairing and in 2021, the *Peach Blossom Star* which has landed firmly in its sector enhances relations between a Rabbit and one of its own sign. Both will be very much in the mood for love, so if there is even a hint of initial attraction, it is easy for sparks to get flying. In 2021, there is a lot of joy and passion for two Rabbits at the start of a romantic relationship. When in each other's arms, you experience a real high, and your connection transcends the physical.

> You tickle each other's minds with your crazy ideas, and two Rabbits will find each other receptive to whatever wild schemes the other has in its head.

Rabbits create loving relationships and happy families with their own kind. They are polite and well-mannered with each other, demonstrating a respect which both appreciate. There is an instinctive understanding and a total absence of competitiveness. This establishes a strong base for a solid relationship to grow.

Over the years, a double Rabbit pairing is likely to become stronger rather than weaken. They live and work on the same wavelength, and between them hostility or misunderstandings rarely arise. The good thing about Rabbits is that they are rarely hostile creatures. To them, the peaceful approach is always to be preferred.

In their household, there is rarely cause for voices to be raised in anger. Should feelings get hurt, this is expressed with studied cool. They do not sulk; they merely adopt an air of super indifference. As a result, little is said and this makes it easier to get back together again once the anger dissipates.

In 2021, the Rabbit enjoys a smooth ride. The young Rabbit just finishing up with studies will face the world with anticipation and excitement. It will be as focused on career as on love, and should they be dating, the year brings a steady relationship with few hassles or difficulties. Marriage may even be on the cards. They only need to watch out for third party intrusion into their idyll as the Peach Blossom brings romance in heavy measure. Older Rabbits enjoy similarly wonderful outlooks when it comes to relationships, and the single older Rabbit may finally find their soulmate.

Two long-married Rabbits may look back and remember this year as one of the "second honeymoon". A wonderful time for love, and for two Rabbits, it's double the love.

RABBIT with DRAGON

Passion and romance await these two!

Rabbit and Dragon have similar tastes and an ability to work well together and although they sometimes see an occasional disagreement, generally, this is a peaceful match which brings happiness and love to both. The Dragon is a dominating kind of person and the Rabbit accepts this, and is in fact attracted to it. These two will have few problems building a nest together as they tend to have a natural preference for the same things. They both belong to the season of Spring, bringing strong growth energy to the relationship.

> In 2021, when Rabbit has the Peach Blossom Star in its sector, this union is blessed not just with shared ideals and ambitions, but passion and romance as well.

Neither Rabbit nor Dragon are the seriously competitive type when it comes to their loved ones. This is a relationship that does not get spoilt by petty or complicated egos clashing. The Rabbit has no problem creating a stable relationship with the Dragon, as both are able to see the big picture and instinctively work towards achieving results they both desire. This makes an excellent basis to create something potentially sound and lasting together.

When it comes to forging a united front when dealing with troublemakers from the outside trying to upset their equilibrium, this pair is also very on the ball. Their loyalty to one another is unmatched, and this is the secret of their resilience and also their happiness. The Dragon can fly as high or as far as it wishes, and the Rabbit is always nearby offering support and a helping hand.

This year, Rabbit enjoys infinitely better luck indications than Dragon, so it gives its powerful friend a leg up. But Rabbit gets inspired by Dragon's untiring vigour and lust for life, because even when hit by the troublesome *Five Yellow*, the passionate Dragon does not let its light get dimmed.

A relationship between Rabbit and Dragon is extremely auspicious for both. The energies of 2021 may see Rabbit playing a more prominent part in the relationship, and their regular roles may get reversed for the time being, with Dragon supporting Rabbit from the sidelines. But the good thing with this union is that neither have a problem with playing second fiddle to the other. If Rabbit and Dragon come together, the truest of love can grow.

RABBIT with SNAKE

Making a fabulous team in 2021

Both Rabbit and Snake are far-sighted individuals who have an intrinsic understanding of the nature of relationships. They will use their good nature and inherent wisdom to make their love or business relationships work, and because they can also be quite tenacious, they are likely to succeed.

These are two signs that can compromise and rationalise really well and they also tend to be rather old-fashioned and traditional. Once committed, Rabbit and Snake will work really hard to make their relationship work. And 2021 may well see these two come together should they meet and sparks fly.

Snake is the pickier of the two when it comes to settling for a partner and entering into any kind of committed relationship, but in 2021, the Rabbit easily ensnares the Snake with the help of its Peach Blossom energies.

Should Rabbit and Snake come together this year, theirs will be a beautiful rapport. They find much in common, and there is much success and joy, making for a magnificent union. The only obstacle facing this pair will be the Snake's *Five Yellow*, but all other indications

point to a wonderful union with little resistance from both sides.

> Rabbit and Snake teaming up in business will do wonderfully well, benefitting from the Rabbit's strong element chi and the Snake's *Big Auspicious* indication. Both have strongly analytical minds and are loyal to their cause, and in a work relationship, neither will allow emotional factors to affect what matters most.

2021 sees these two getting along like a house on fire, so conflicts will be few and far between. There will be many laughs along the way, and even if they meet up with obstacles along the way, their good humour sees them weather them and laugh afterwards.

This is a hugely warm and heartfelt relationship. When one suffers from any kind of temporary poor luck, the other will prop it up no questions asked. Their relationship is never calculative, so neither side keeps count who does more for the other. This allows the union to work on any level, whether in love, at work, at home or at play.

RABBIT with HORSE

Attraction grows in 2021

The Rabbit and Horse share a natural love bond. The Rabbit is the *Peach Blossom Animal* of the Horse, so attraction between these two comes very naturally. Even though their personalities and interests differ considerably, there is a special spark that gets lit between them that cannot be explained.

In this pairing, Rabbit willingly follows the adventurous Horse on a joyride, and when together, fun and happiness flows effortlessly! Time spent together is never boring, and there is genuine devotion felt on both sides.

In 2021, the year's energies bring these two together, with the Rabbit's Peach Blossom joining with Horse's Victory Star to conjure up a storm of love vibes. Passion flows freely with each sweeping the other off its feet!

2021 promises to be a wonderful time for a Rabbit and Horse pairing, especially if they come together in a romantic setting. Horse's energetic nature breathes life into the more sedate Rabbit, bringing out its passionate and carefree side. Around a Horse, Rabbit feels free and able to conquer the world. Horse meanwhile easily falls head over heels for the demure Rabbit, who oozes passion this year under the spell of the *Peach Blossom*.

This union works especially well if you are in the budding stages of your relationship. Those who have only just met have many adventures to look forward to and the attraction each feels for the other grows stronger as the year progress.

But for those who have been involved with each other for a while, they need to watch out for third parties who may interfere with their heady mix of romance. Temptation is everywhere, especially for the Rabbit, so for the pairing to last, Horse needs to stay devoted, interested and vigilant.

This year, the energies are strongly positive for these two, helping the relationship blossom and flourish, but when the year is over, whether they stay together or not will depend on many other things. They may make a passionate pairing but the attraction can be superficial.

Unless there are common interests and goals, the fire may not burn quite so bright once the magic of 2021 comes to a close.

RABBIT with SHEEP

Much love between two soulmates

Rabbit and Sheep are two kindred spirits able to really wax lyrical about all the finer things in life and enjoy them together. This is a couple who are sure to work out well, as they find beauty and value in exactly the same things. It is like they are of one mind when they indulge themselves. They are like a match made in heaven making beautiful music together.

They get their highs discovering new experiences together and are able to create their own world where love flows very freely. They get bored at the same kinds of things and are stimulated by similar experiences. So here we see an emotional and artistic affinity flowering into deep and abiding love. This couple are certain to become soul mates capable of bringing great happiness to each other.

2021 sees Rabbit in the mood for romance, while Sheep has the quarrelsome star affliction. But in each other's arms, the cares of the world melt away and they constantly lift each other's spirits.

Rabbit may have to work a bit harder in light of Sheep's pricklier disposition in 2021, but with these two, arguments usually get put out before they grow into anything big. If Sheep is mad with the world, rather than fight with a Rabbit partner, Rabbit is more likely to jump to Sheep's defence and they fight the sins of the world together. They are there for each other through thick and thin, and they forgive each other anything.

These two are genuine allies, looking out for each other and creating easy rapport and comradeship.

Whether the relationship is a romantic or platonic one, there is always great warmth and affection. As work colleagues or business partners, they get along like a house on fire, so it rarely feels like work. But they can be mighty productive together, as both are responsible types who do not let distractions affect productivity.

As workmates, there is risk this year of Rabbit and Sheep hooking up romantically but illicitly. If each are separately happily married to other people, a passionate affair may lead to emotional complications, not to mention professional ones, so it is a good idea to be aware of such risks. They will enjoy it for sure, but an illicit tryst may not be worth endangering everything for. And don't think it will be a casual one-time fling, because between these two, once something begins, it will not just end. Their connection runs too deep for that.

RABBIT with MONKEY

An uneven relationship

A Rabbit and Monkey relationship can work, especially in the short term, but there is so little in common that this rarely makes a solid pairing in the long run. The problem stems from this being an extremely uneven relationship, one which brings few benefits to the Rabbit. Here the Monkey is so completely in charge and the Rabbit so smitten that it can become a horribly one-sided union.

In this pairing, Rabbit is simply too mesmerized by the Monkey and this can be unhealthy, especially when Monkey is the sole bread winner. Here the view from the Rabbit's perspective is that Monkey is simply irresistible who can do no wrong. As long as Monkey stays faithful to the Rabbit, there should be little problem. It is only when the flirtatious Monkey starts to develop a roving eye that potential heartbreak and depression can set in.

Even when this couple are able to sustain a long-term relationship it is only because of the tolerance and patience of the Rabbit who will be the one giving in and swallowing whatever nonsense is being dished out by the Monkey. So potentially, this is a pairing that does not bring much happiness to the Rabbit so no matter how smart and debonair the Monkey, it is better in the long-run for the Rabbit to resist the Monkey's charms and look elsewhere for long-term commitments.

In 2021, the Rabbit has the *Peach Blossom Star* which makes it extremely attractive to whoever it gets involved with. The Monkey on the other hand is afflicted by the *Quarrelsome Star*, making it irritable and difficult to get along with. But if the two have only just met, initial attraction can blind them to the truth of the matter. They are just not all that compatible.

> Rabbit has strong chi energy this year, but so does the Monkey. The union will work so long as Rabbit is prepared to put up with Monkey's cavalier ways, and while Monkey stays enamoured with the alluring Rabbit. But their relationship is built on such shaky ground that it only takes a little for what happiness they have to fall apart.

These two are not naturally made for each other. They do not share similar life views nor do they think the same way. Their relationship is completely dependent on them not knowing each other too well, so once the honeymoon period is over, the relationship may venture onto very rocky footing. The advice is not to fall in love, or heartbreak may follow.

RABBIT with ROOSTER

A mismatched union hostile as ever

These two cardinal signs are natural adversaries of the zodiac, and between them, there can never be true love or affection. While they may get along on first meeting, with seemingly much in common, they can be superficial friends at best, because as soon as they go any deeper, serious doubts and misgivings arise.

From the way they think to the way they work, they have vastly different styles and attitudes. Rabbit occupies the East, the place of the rising Sun, while Rooster rules the West, the direction of the setting sun. In terms of their attitudes, one is naturally positive and hopeful, while the other tends to be morose and meloancholy. The Rabbit is symptomatic of Spring when new shoots appear, and the Rooster is diametrically opposite, representing the sober realities of the Fall season which heralds the coming of Winter.

This pair cannot see eye-to-eye. They are unlikely to last whether as a couple, business partners or even best friends.

When Rabbit and Rooster come together and their relationship becomes too deep, they bring nothing but heartache to one another. There may well be initial sparks of attraction, as both are passionate creatures, but in the end, one will hurt or destroy the other. Note that their elements are Wood for the Rabbit and Metal for the Rooster, so here Wood gets cut by Metal. Their elements are not in sync, and while the loving energies of 2021 may hide some of the deep differences between them, as the year unfolds, these differences will only become more pronounced.

> If a Rabbit and Rooster are already married and started out in love, to keep the honeymoon going the best way is to create the special relationship cross of signs that bring good fortune by having two children, one born in the year of the Horse and one born in the year of the Rat. This creates what feng shui experts refer to as the *Cardinal Cross*.

This brings power and fame for the family and the balance that gets created is caused by the tension strings formed by these two pairs of "enemy signs", except that as a cross, they indicate excellent good fortune. You can also display this **Cardinal Cross** as a feng shui cure. If you are in business together, best to use intermediaries to ensure you do not get too close. Or add two key employees one born in the year of the Rat and the other in the year of the Horse.

RABBIT with DOG
So good for each other

Rabbit and Dog are always good for each other. They are secret friends of the Zodiac, so if they find one another, their relationship can quickly develop into great affection and deep love. The Rabbit in 2021 has all the energies of the *Peach Blossom* behind it, making it extremely attractive to others, and a Dog that crosses its path will hardly be able to resist.

> The beautiful thing about a Rabbit and Dog pairing is their wonderful simpatico. They forgive each other's misgiving, almost blind to each other's faults, so when together, they bring out all that is good in one another.

The Dog in 2021 comes under the influence of the *Loss Star*, so it may not be going through the easiest of times, but with a Rabbit partner, the Dog grows strong and resilient. Rabbit falls in love easily this year, and with a Dog, it gains a partner who appreciates it for who it is. Their love for each other is thus incredibly and enduring.

When Rabbit and Dog succeed in getting married, theirs will be a satisfying life with the promise of great happiness. Even if they should separate or part for any reason, this is a couple who will usually stay good friends.

Rabbit and Dog can rely on each other in good times or bad, and the compatibility of their feelings and attitudes override all obstacles. Any attempt to split them up or introduce suspicion between them is unlikely to work, and in 2021, Rabbit pulls Dog out of its troublesome periods.

As work mates or business partners, they look out for one another and there is a great deal of trust. They bring out all that is creative in each other and there is a lot of mutual respect. The luck of the Rabbit trumps that of the Dog this year, so in this pair, it is likely that Rabbit will take the lead. Dog however is happy to follow without grumbls or complaint. Theirs is a partnership of equals, because even when one side agrees for the other to take the lead, its opinions are always carefully considered.

They make great friends and confidantes to each other, and their conversations are always relaxed and easy-going. Should they come together as a couple, not only will their union be a happy one, they bring much success luck to one another as well.

RABBIT with BOAR

Made for each other

Rabbit and Boar make a very happy couple who are extremely well-suited. In fact, they are one of the very best matches in the Chinese Zodiac. There is an enthusiastic approach to life that is inspiring to watch and infectious. This pair rings happiness to those around them, as their obvious love for each other makes being with them both restful and easy. They are soulmates loving the same things and being motivated by the same kind of people, situations and attainments.

Their aspirations are in line with each other's, so as a couple, it is easy for them to make plans. If they get into a work relationship, they amalgamate their thoughts and efforts very well. Outsiders will find it difficult to cause friction between them because they have a strong and durable bond.

In 2021, Rabbit's Peach Blossom Energy puts it in the mood for love; and in the arms of the enchanting Boar, it finds plenty of that and more.

While the Boar has to contend with the *Loss Star* in its sector, with a Rabbit by its side, all its trials and tribulations become easier to bear. The Boar enjoys two *Auspicious Stars* from the 24 mountains, but it suffers

from very weak element luck. So it lacks the energy it needs to effectively capture the opportunities coming its way. But with a Rabbit mate, everything becomes easier. Rabbit gives Boar the confidence and staying power it needs to go after its dreams, and as a pair, whatever one aspires after, the other can makes it its dream as well.

> Rabbit and Boar can build a beautiful friendship, and if they fall in love, a very happy and fulfilling family life together. With these two, there is rarely any angst and little conflict. It is an extremely happy pairing characterised by a quiet elegance.

Neither are clingy or needy types, so they lead very healthy lives alongside the one they share with each other. They do not suffocate each other, yet when they are together, they cannot get enough of one another.

This is a pairing that has the best of everything. Their natural affinity ensures that should they commit themselves to one another, their union will last a long time. This is a wonderful year for Rabbit and Boar in the courting stage to get married, or to take their relationship to the next level. If they find themselves in love, this relationship is worth putting in every effort for.

Rabbit's Monthly Horoscope 2021

Chapter 6

Love & relationships rule the luck of the Rabbit

The Rabbit emerges in 2021 much stronger and more optimistic, and its stakes in the love game improves big time! Your popularity with friends and relatives gets a big boost, a great relief from last year when you were afflicted by the troublesome Five Yellow. Your social life brings much joy, attracting love and inspiration from all quarters. You may find yourself rekindling old friendships, mending relationships that went a bit wobbly last year, and everyone you meet acts more kindly towards you. Those looking for love should open your hearts and accept all the loving vibes coming your way!

1st Month
February 4th - March 5th 2021

NOISY START TO THE YEAR

The quarrelsome star afflicts the Rabbit as the year gets off to a whipping start. While you are feeling energized and ready to rumble, this month sees your irritable side surface a little too often. Make an effort to control your temper, as quarrelling with the wrong people could set you back quite a few steps. This is a year when relationships become especially important for the Rabbit, and you don't want to be burning bridges so early on in the year. When you feel your hackles rising, take time out rather than react on impulse. The Rabbit is a naturally diplomatic sign, but when pushed to the wall, your reflex reaction may be the kind you will regret. This month then, the most important advice is to consider your words before you utter them.

Work & Career - *Go with the flow*

Best thing to do this month is go with the flow. Instead of being dogmatic and sticking to your opinions and what you feel is right, it is better for all parties if you are more pliant, going with the flow instead of resisting. If you are forced into a corner, resist the temptation of fighting with your colleagues. They seem too many in number and too concerted as a group for you to win.

Try not to disagree or push your point across if there is no real reason. Try wearing more of the **colour red**; this shade tones down your temper and aggression, as it burns up the afflicted quarrelsome energies which are Wood element in nature. This seems to be a busy month and career luck continues to be good, but not fantastic, so save your grand ideas for another time. If you tend to slack, forget it! Coming in late or vanishing before official work hours are over will be noted. Be punctual efficient and play by the rules.

A quarrelsome month for the Rabbit, so be careful. Little things annoy you, but reacting will only make things worse. Make every effort to keep calm!

Business - *Miscommunications*

The most pressing problems come from misunderstandings so when you find yourself in this unenviable position, try making your stand clear. Let everyone know your stance from the beginning so no miscommunication can occur. The air of hostility seems pervasive and hard to dispel, so try living with it. Your charm levels are at a low ebb and try as you might, you appear less than attractive compared to your usual gregarious, popular self. Don't worry; this is temporary. Avoid closing big deals or selling big projects; your ideas, however realistic, seem to lack appeal. If there are important pitches, let others do the job for you.

Your presentations may fall flat, so don't chance it. Be meticulous with paperwork lest misunderstandings occur. It could be something as simple as a comma or full stop or it could be a serious factual error. Whatever the case, you are held responsible, so double check everything connected to the legal department. Stay firmly within the law; if you break any, the long arm of the law will get you even if it is not criminal in nature.

Love & Relationships - *Argumentative*

A bad month for relationships, so brace yourself for a multitude of hassles. Even if you are tolerant and bend backwards to please your partner, petty arguments can still blow into cyclonic proportions. Saying too much is a bad idea let alone criticizing others. If you have nothing nice to say, keep silent.

> **CURE FOR THE MONTH:** Carry the **Apple Peace Amulet** this month. Clip onto your bag or use as a keychain.

School & Education - *Tensions*

Problems with teachers come to a head as tensions reach boiling point. If you get into trouble with teachers, guess who will be at the losing end? You may feel rebellious and wish to impose your will on those around you, even if it involves bending the rules. Don't. Not only will you fail in your quest for world domination, you will be caught and punished.

2nd Month
March 6th - April 4th 2021

BUSY MONTH WITH LOTS TO DO

The Rabbit's energy levels get sapped this month. You are kept constantly on the move and even when you clear your schedule for some precious "me" time, something crops up to get you busy again. The #2 star in your chart puts a dampener on your usual Energizer Rabbit self, so you are just not as lively as usual to cope with so much stimulation from all corners. Take a step back if it all becomes too much. Often, it doesn't take much time to recharge, but you do have to actively tell yourself to switch off. In today's hectic world, it is all too easy to let yourself get overwhelmed, and this is one of those months when your brain is in serious need of a reboot. Taking a short holiday will do you wonders.

Work & Career - *Don't sweat the small stuff*
Your mental and physical states are weak. You are wallowing in the doldrums so you should not work such long hours nor exert yourself too much, since body and soul cannot take it. Work smart and fill your days with productive results. Do not slave over minor details that do not count much. Allow others in and

don't be too worried about claiming credit. You need assistance to get the job done! Having the right people on your side will do wonders and benefit your career now and in the near future.

You may feel weak but you still wield power. Just don't let your arrogance get the better of you. You need much goodwill these days, and so appearing modest and less self-serving will be a good start.

Business - *Be bold with business plans*
Money luck is with you but you should focus on just one or two things. If you spread yourself too thin, you may not have the energy to see them through. Why begin something you cannot finish properly? Having projects stuck halfway is worse than having nothing since they may return to haunt you or threaten you with more monetary outlay. Be bold with your business plans as this month, fortune favours the bold this month. Being bold is not the same as being reckless, so differentiate between the two! You can get carried away by the first signs of success and think you can start laughing all the way to the bank. Still, you can take some risks as you are particularly investment savvy this month, so chances are high that whatever you touch can turn gold.

Love & Relationships - *Many admirers*

Single Rabbits find love easily and with little effort. You have lots of admirers and should accept invites to parties and indulge in some more serious socializing. After all the wear and tear at the office, this is a welcome respite. But don't rush into a steady relationships yet, as most are ships sailing through the night. Still, as long as you have fun and enjoy the company, you should savour the moment.

Health & Wellness - *Take care of yourself*

Illness and accidents loom in the horizon so beware and take the necessary steps to offset potential problems. Watch out for your health by taking things easy. Safer and less problematic to err on caution. More so when you get tired easily. If so, make sure you get ample rest. Health is wealth and you enjoy a good measure of money luck. But sometimes if an infusion of cash is saddled with ill health, it may not be worth it.

Education - *Help from a mentor*

Young Rabbits at school fare well but need a mentor or guide. This can be a teacher, student or even someone who has graduated from the school earlier. The Rabbit kid benefits much from a mentor figure this month.

CURE FOR THE MONTH: Carry the **Health Talisman Holder** with Medicine Buddha and Vairocana mantras to protect against falling sick, and boost mentor luck with the **Gui Ren Talisman**.

3rd Month
April 5th - May 5th 2021

WINNING LUCK
PUTS YOU AHEAD OF COMPETITION

Your good fortune luck starts rocking in this month with the appearance of the Victory Star. This is the start of a whole run of excellent months, so you can feel confident starting new projects, getting going on initiatives and being generally brasher, bolder and less tentative. Take the bull by the horns and go pursue those big dreams of yours! In any form of contest or competition, victory comes easily! You have what they call "winning luck". Whether you are literally in a competition, contesting for a promotion at work, fighting for bigger market share in business, good fortune luck smiles upon you. A month which heralds some changes in your life, but all for the better! Very happy times ahead!

Work & Career - *Feeling strong*

You are in an independent mood and want things done your way. You feel physically strong, so this may cloud your judgment, but hold back on the tendency to control everyone and do everything yourself. Work at being a better team member, more so when you already are one! Trying to usurp those in authority and going it alone may backfire as you could discover you have pushed yourself out of the picture!

If your work involves research, you do particularly well as this is a period of discovery for you.

Something you discover in the course of research can have a great bearing on your career, so bear this in mind. If thinking of a job change, this is a fortuitous time, since a move augurs well. If you receive a tempting job offer, don't hesitate too long! Take the leap and reap the rewards.

Business - *New strategies*

If you are the boss, this is the best time to begin something new as anything fresh and innovative stands a great chance of being a success. So be bold and aim high. Think up new initiatives, strategies, products and even new launches. Anything upbeat and optimistic seems to be able to bear fruit quickly. Changes made this month will be good decisions, as luck is on your side. A good time for partnerships though you think you are in a position to dominate the deal. Do so if you can get away with it since the stakes are stacked in your favour. But some may be put off by your domineering attitude, so beware.

Love & Relationships - *Finding a soulmate*

There is a great deal of romance, but you need make the effort and take the initiative. If not, things stagnate or worse, fall apart. You tend to treat your partner lightly and be superficial in your outlook. This may work against you so try to be more loving and sincere. New friendships get formed quickly, and those of you looking for love may finally decide you've found your soulmate. If you have, make your move. Don't let life pass you by. Go for it!

Friends & Family - *Change it up*

A change of routine can be beneficial. Apart from alleviating boredom, a new routine will add zest to family life. You also enjoy the company of your children and they will love the extra time you devote to them.

Education - *Going great guns*

Study luck is strong so you can splash out on a social life and get away with it. Hanging out with friends can be delightful distractions but make sure they do not intrude too much into your academic juggernaut. However, all is going so well for you there is little to worry and plenty to enjoy. Sometimes you plough in so much effort only to reap minor rewards, but this is the time when an average time spent on studies seems to push you skyhigh!

> **ENHANCER FOR THE MONTH:** Carry the **Victory Banner Success Amulet** or **Windhorse Success Amulet** this month.

4th Month
May 6th - June 5th 2021

NEW BUSINESS OPPORTUNITIES

The month ahead marks a second month running this year when the Rabbit's luck holds very strong. The *Business Ho Tu* combination that forms in your sector brings you business and commercial success. You enjoy an unprecedented burst of energy, so much and in such doses that you seem positively electrified. Even those around you are influenced by your renewed enthusiasm and energy and are inspired to try and match you. This is a busy time with plenty on your plate, so it is a godsend you have the necessary physical and mental strength to see them through. You are like a fully wound-up automaton let loose. You won't be able to stay still, let alone sit till the tasks are done! Just watch you don't overdo things. If you spread yourself too thin, you could end up not doing yourself full justice.

Work & Career - *Sweet Talker*

No surprises if you are the sweet talker of the office and can outtalk anyone with your knowledge and some juicy insider information. No one can beat the Rabbit with vocal eloquence. and this month your skills here get enhanced. But be careful; too much talk can land you in trouble with the powers that be. Don't try to appear too smart as you may ruffle some feathers!

Good time for laying foundation work. By putting in hard work now, you stand to reap big dividends in the near future.

Business - *Building for the future*
A month laden with plenty of good ideas that enhance your cash flow. You are fortunate as your solid team of capable workers are backing you up making sure all your ideas are enforced and productive! This is also a good time to hire new staff and take in young recruits, as one or more will later prove to be of great worth. Upping the staff level now augurs well. Since this is a news-making month, those involved in activities that generate publicity will do well. Politicians, actors, singers, models, designers and entertainers benefit. Money luck may appear sluggish till next month, but hang in there, as things are fast improving. Persevere.

ENHANCER FOR THE MONTH: Display the **Ho Tu Enhancer Mirror** in the East to empower the auspicious business Ho Tu in your chart. Keep the **"Green Dragon" Constellation Lucky Charms** near you to get timing right when it comes to strategic moves and decisions.

Love & Relationships - *Relax!*

Let your hair down and let it rip! The less uptight you
are, the easier for you to find true love. Look on the
bright side and improve your sense of humour. Life
becomes not only easier but more fun that way. Single
Rabbits are poised to find their soulmate, so hang in
there and keep looking. For those married among you,
even if your partner cannot cope with your excess
energy, you are considerate and more giving than
usual, so all augurs well here. Good time for a holiday,
even a short one; taking one with your spouse could
rekindle some of those old flames that seem to simmer
beneath the surface.

Home & Family - *Make time*

You are so busy with your burgeoning career that your
family may be relegated right to the back of your mind.
This is no good. Try and find time to relax with them
since they are the ones indirectly giving you moral or
spiritual support. If you use your family as a sounding
board, they may provide just the solution you needed
or were looking for.

Education - *Get the ball rolling*

The more you do, the happier and more satisfied
you get. The more your study, the easier everything
becomes. It works like a multiplier effect on the young
Rabbit. Getting the ball rolling will be the hardest part;
after that, everything falls into place.

5th Month
June 6th - July 6th 2021

OPPORTUNITIES TO MAKE MONEY

Another fantastic month for the Rabbit! New opportunities to augment wealth come along. Additional income streams get added seamlessly and by chance. Take every new suggestion that comes your way seriously. Your good fortune luck holds, so you can afford to be more bullish on new investments. You are in high gear mode and not only do you move naturally and confidently ahead with your plans, you are able to influence others to feel the same. A good time for important ceremonies like signing documents, treaties, openings and other important events. Enjoy all you can this month, as nothing lasts forever. The saying make hay while the sun shines has never been more apt. Stay industrious!

Work & Career - *Impressing the right people*
A big break may come along, so keep your eyes peeled for opportunities. Work on your relationships; someone is in a position to really improve your career. Impressing the right people is especially fruitful. Your luck crystalises this month, so work on it. You begin to see the fruits of your labour and appreciate the

time and effort you put in earlier. The results from
your hard work will inspire you further as you aim
even higher. Your natural talents shine through as
colleagues and bosses are amply reminded of what
you have done and can continue to do to improve the
company's bottom-line. You get plenty of pats on the
back as congratulations pour in. Don't let the bouquets
get to your head. Always remember the brickbats are a
bouquet's consort.

*A month when good fortune flows in from
many directions. Keep up the momentum
while luck is so firmly on your side.*

Business - *Sparkling*

The perfect time to sign deals, close contracts and
finalise all the fine print. Everything seems to be
going your way and people give in to you however
outrageous your demands. While they submit to you
now, be gracious and generous or they will hold this
against you when times are bad. All the agreements
you make now will bear fruit quickly and last for a
reasonably long time, so this may well be your heritage
to pass on. Since people make or break your business,
be sociable as you are the pole star with many eager to
gather round you. Your sparkling persona will make
you a hit at gatherings, from corporate to cocktail.

ENHANCER FOR THE MONTH: Carry the **Pi Yao Wealth Amulet** or the **Pi Yao Wealth Gold Talisman Card** in your wallet to tap the wealth energies brought by the *Prosperity Star* this month.

Love & Relationships - *Sights on the future*

While dating and flirting is fun, the single Rabbit will be more interested in long term relationships than short term flings. A roll in the haystack holds little appeal now as your thoughts settle more firmly on the future. If you're currently with someone you cannot see yourself ending up with, you're likely to want out. Don't shy away from becoming single again; when you want good things to come into your life, you need to make room. Even if it means ending a current relationship that is no longer working. For the married Rabbit, you appreciate your partner more and more as all their good qualities become obvious. Previously you may have taken them for granted but now you realize you are the lucky one. As you show your concern, it is more than reciprocated.

Education - *All-round*

An easy time for Rabbits in school. Things are going your way and accumulating new knowledge is no sweat. Some may gain a leadership position this month. Your mainstream work is going well so start thinking also of building up your extrecurricular *resume*.

6th Month
July 7th - Aug 7th 2021

BEWARE BETRAYALS
BY THOSE CLOSE TO YOU

The energies this month bring danger of burglary, loss of money and being cheated by people you think you know well. Don't be too trusting. Betrayals come from unexpected sources, sometimes without ill intent on the perpetrators' part. Don't expose yourself to risk. Better lie low than forge on with any grand plans. Use the month to step back and look at the big picture. Re-strategise and think of new ways to implement ideas for future. Avoid late nights; if you must go out, try to be home before midnight and be extra careful. Do not pick a fight as some people are egging you on for that very purpose. You may not know who you are up against, so keep a low profile.

Work & Career - *Workplace politics*

Don't expose yourself where you can be criticized as you are in a vulnerable position and open to downgrades. Keep your thoughts close to your chest; if anyone knows your current weaknesses, they can be exploited against you. Competition is fierce amidst office politicking and you are in a weakened position,

so be careful who you side and confide in. Don't share
private secrets to anyone.

CURE FOR THE MONTH: Display a
Rooster with Crown on your work desk
to protect against office politics and being
outplayed by rivals at work.

Stay put in your corner and work hard.
Do your job well and hope it gets
noticed. Recognition will only come later,
so don't get your hopes up.

Business - Damage control

You may get swindled. While you may think this is
the last thing you will allow to happen, even the most
hardened tycoons get cheated, so this is just another sad
fact of life. Best thing this month is not to trust others
too easily. If you do find something amiss and catch the
culprit red-handed, avoid direct confrontation. Save
any public accusation for another time. For now, just do
damage control. Some investments or purchases made
some time ago may turn sour and you end up with
a loss. If the loss is minimal or manageable, let it be.
Do not interfere in other people's affairs or problems.
You are in no position to help. If you can maintain the
current status quo, you should thank your stars. Don't
over invest and don't overspend. Conserve both money
and energy for later.

Love & Relationships - *Taking a back seat*

Keep yourself to yourself and don't send out the wrong
vibes as you seem to be attracting all the wrong people
right now. Love takes a back seat so you should bear
this in mind if your love life is on the back burner.
Minor disagreements have a tendency to get blown
up into bigger issues, so nip them in the bud. If not,
more people get pulled into your personal life when
you need peace and quiet. Those married but going
through a rocky time here should carry the **Enhancing
Relationships Amulet** to fend off any risk of infidelities.
It will also stop you from making a bad mistake.

Friendships - *Difficult*

Friendships get rather edgy. You fight for no reason and
you hardly know who to trust. Best to keep to yourself
and don't reveal too much. Avoid gossiping. The less
said the better.

Education - *Conflict*

Conflict with a teacher or another student could happen.
Don't harp on an issue when everyone else considers it
dead and buried. You do not need to have the last word.
Keep on and you could lose yourself a few friends. Some
pals may upset you, as they seem to betray your trust,
but take it easy. Give them the benefit of the doubt.
Their actions may not have been intentional. Don't
throw away a friendship over something small, and in
the bigger scheme of things, meaningless.

7th Month
Aug 8th - Sept 7th 2021

PLENTY OF GOOD FORTUNE FROM THE HEAVENS!

A wonderful month when everything goes your way! The Rabbit enjoys a visit from the *Heaven Star,* which combines with the annual #4 to form the very auspicious Sum-of-Ten. A great time for work and money. People are happy to listen to you and completion luck is on the upswing. Projects get completed ahead of schedule, so you are in a good mood. You enjoy mentor luck too with people in high places helping you. Someone unexpected may emerge and play an influential role. He or she will be a guiding light and be a blessing to your prospects. The determined Rabbit will do very well as the stars are aligned in your favour.

Work & Career - *Ignore criticisms*

You easily get what you want, so go for it. Reach high, aim directly for your target, no need for any circuitous routes. Ignore criticisms if you encounter any; if you think they don't exist, they can't affect you. There is some competition but nothing that you cannot handle. Surround yourself with people who make you feel good about yourself. You don't deal well with criticism right now. And why should you. You are on a roll. Remove all threats to your success, which, if achieved, promises to be pretty big!

If things are sailing along nicely, don't rock the boat. The Heavens have chartered out an enviable path for you, so trust in the universe. Learn to go with the flow and enjoy the goodies that come your way.

Business - *Connections*

Wealth luck is flowing in and you are reaping the rewards. Easy money comes in the form of some windfall. Embrace the opportunities falling into your lap. This streak of good luck you have stumbled upon has the potential to continue and grow, so don't stop now. Think bigger than you already do. Someone with the power to help you could enter your life soon. Don't dismiss help offered even if it manifests in an unexpected form. Listen to advice given; even if you do not follow it verbatim, it will get you thinking and help you make better decisions. Be brave in your endeavours but listen to what others have to say. If you need connections to get things done, you are able to do so as you now have some powerful strings to pull. This is the time to call for favours as it's payback time! Have the **Gui Ren Talisman Plaque** on your workdesk. This engages the support of the *Jade Emperor* and enhances the quality of mentor luck helping you.

Love & Relationships - *Good times!*

A groovy month for love and you are in the right form too! Physically and mentally, you are in the mood for love. One of you will tend to be dominant in the relationship but both will enjoy, so don't treat it as a challenge for pole position. Discover something new as a couple as you may find both share a hitherto unknown skill, talent or interest in a hobby. Singles waiting to make the first move can do so now as the object of your desire seems receptive to your approaches. This is the right time to flirt as a new relationship is waiting to happen!

Friendships - *Entertain*

Invite a friend or two over for dinner and drinks. Entertain at home whether on small or large scale. Strengthening your connections brings unexpected benefits. Information you glean can be surprisingly useful to you, and relationships you fortify could prove remarkably advantageous.

Education - *Mentor luck*

A great time to start scouting for a mentor figure who can be a teacher or older student in a higher grade than you. They will help you when you need it most. In school, the more you actively participate, the better you do.

ENHANCER FOR THE MONTH: Carry the **Sum-of-Ten Amulet** to capture the extremely auspicious energies of the month.

8th Month
Sept 8th - Oct 7th 2021

MISFORTUNE STAR WREAKS HAVOC

Not a good month for business or socializing as people get on your nerves just as you have a tendency to irritate them too! Luck is far away so lie low, stay quiet and do not attract too much attention. Any light shining on you tends to show up your faults and weaknesses! The Five Yellow has landed in your sector, conjuring up all kinds of obstacles for you. This is a temporary aberration in your luck; even so, don't let bad decisions you make at this time snowball into something you cannot contain. If you are unsure of your next move, better to hesitate and do nothing. Leave big decisions to next month when you won't be clouded by so much indecision or self-doubt. Avoid reacting on impulse.

Work & Career - *Status Quo*

A bad time to make any major move like getting a new job, moving house or getting married! Even if you have a tempting job offer, better to stay put and remain where you are. If the job offer entails moving to another town, it is even worse. Stick to what you are doing. As it is, you are struggling to maintain the status quo, so if you

are too ambitious, it will backfire. Any big decisions
made now will end in grief, so postpone anything major.
In fact, look at this period as one of rest, since whatever
you do can't seem to hit the target. Stay low key and if
you have some leave left, consider a holiday! A break
from office routine seems the most beneficial thing you
can do for yourself, saving you from more grouses from
the boss.

Business - *Stay cautious*

Be conservative as traditionalists win out this month.
Be prudent and do things by the book and you will not
go far wrong. Too arrogant an attitude and everything
you do will backfire. Opportunities are slow so take
things easy, since luck is not on your side. Carry on
with business based on the status quo. Don't make big
changes as they will have a detrimental effect instead of
improving the bottom line. Your luck this month is not
good, so stay within limits as you are in no position to
test them.

> *Avoid any kind of speculative plays this
> month, you may not be able to survive the
> losses.*

Love & Relationships - *Not feeling the love*

Love seems second place and out of your life and you
don't even seem to mind! In fact, you may take the
initiative to be alone! You feel like being by yourself and

may let your partner down and not feel guilty. Worse, you may fall out of love altogether as being lovey-dovey now just grates on your nerves. If the union is important to you, do not do anything rash or foolish. Be the bigger person and just don't upset the status quo. It is not that bad when you can just take things easy.

Home & Family - *Stifling*

While you may love your family dearly, somehow the sight of them fails to arouse much empathy or compassion now. Indeed, too much time spent with those closest to you can become stifling. If you feel like you are being suffocated from all sides due to unreasonable demands, you should spend time away. Don't make things worse by trying to patch up fights that become even bigger fights. A little time out may be just what you need.

Education - *Feeling vulnerable*

Things don't seem to work out in your favour at this time and studies are slow. All these compound your sense of doom and gloom. You become more sensitive and thin-skinned. If there is someone who makes you feel small in any way, avoid that person like the plague! You need some good news to perk you up, not someone pointing out your faults for the world to notice.

CURE FOR THE MONTH: The Rabbit needs to carry the **Five Element Pagoda with Tree of Life Amulet** this month. This is the best cure to suppress the frustrating effects of the #5 star.

9th Month
Oct 8th - Nov 6th 2021

ROMANTIC LIAISONS APLENTY. BEWARE INFIDELITIES.

The month ahead is all about love and romance. Relationships form a much bigger part of your days, and single Rabbits can expect to be swept off their feet! Go ahead and enjoy, but don't commit yourself to any one person too soon. Settling down could be too stifling for all the energy you seem to radiate right now. A better time awaits those of you not already spoken for. If married, watch for the *External Star of Romance*. Better work at rekindling what you have with your spouse; the energies are filled with romance but bring risk of infidelities for marriages that have fallen victim to the ravages of time. An easy month to rekindle dull flames if you put in a little effort.

Work & Career - *Energetic*

A series of happy coincidences allow you to assert your authority with minimal effort. A rare period when things seem to happen as you think about them. Someone you are trying desperately to reach could phone out of the blue or some information you require pops up as you click away at your computer. Teamwork swells as things get done fast, but don't push your team mates too much, as not everyone can keep up with your newfound energy. Share your ideas as they occur as they will be well received, and besides, you tend to forget them if not noted! Focus on relationships with those you work with - your lively rapport with your workmates is what will make all the difference this month. Beware however of office romances - could lead somewhere you regret.

Your creativity is surging and you conjure up ideas nonstop. Many admire you for this wellspring of ideas as most seem to be workable and applicable instantly.

Business - *Networking benefits*

Successful networking nets you immense benefits, so work on this! Life is easy as moneymaking opportunities come from several sources, so you don't have to worry over which way to turn or what step to take. If you have a lead, act on it as it can bring fat rewards. Someone you meet casually can be very beneficial, so do not dismiss unexpected acquaintances. Informal chats unrelated to work could glean you important information or lead to invaluable contacts being formed. Sometimes a chance encounter or innocent phone call just to touch base can have a major role to play in your corporate life. You don't get where you are by sitting alone reading the financial papers. Networking and personal contacts are what can make all the difference for you this month.

Love & Relationships - *Sizzling hot*

A fabulous month for singles looking for love and a relationship. Even if you are attached, your partner is the one making all the effort to please and charm you. If your lust matches your partner's, then this month sizzles like fireworks going off! You should try to be more passionate and show your feelings, as a third party may be lurking in the shadows. If you are holding back and not being demonstrative, your rival may gain ground as your partner's eyes begin to roam and be more receptive to other overtures.

> **CURE FOR THE MONTH:** A passionate month but the *External Flower of Romance* may career out of control. Those happily married should carry the **Enhancing Relationships Amulet** if anything seems amiss. For singles looking to get hitched, boost your luck here with your **Peach Blossom Animal the Rat** placed in the North.

Education - *Much to contribute*

You are eloquent and talkative and totally in chat mode. Nothing wrong in being communicative and getting along with everyone. In fact, your communicating skills this month prove very productive and will help you score extra points. A pleasant and productive period all round when others value your ideas, so keep them coming.

10th Month
Nov 7th - Dec 6th 2021

CONFLICT ENERGIES GET YOU DOWN

A quarrelsome month when the #3 shows up and sends your life into a tailspin. Your irritable mood does not help, so keep your temper in check. Infighting with colleagues, friends and superiors really foul up the month, but these things are sent to test one's patience, so stick your chin up and be resolute. Nothing is as bad as you think. There are risks of lawsuits and legal entanglements; try resolve them out of court and avoid full frontal confrontation as you may lose since your enemies are stronger. Stick strictly within the law. Some temptations for easy money are out there, but if even if it is a grey area, you will be caught and lose out. Don't take that kind of risk.

Work & Career - *Office politics*

You are easily irritated by other people's lack of consistency or what you deem as incompetence. Yet you are banging your head on a brick wall. Even if they are incompetent and inept, they will triumph! Flying off the handle and admonishing them publicly will do no good. It reflects badly on you while the guilty party gets off scot-free! This rubs more salt into your wounds!

Control your temper and beware office politics. So much unnecessary gossip is going on. You know they are time wasting and even if they do not concern you, careless talk and ill-will may get you into hot soup.

> **CURE FOR THE MONTH:** The Rabbit needs to keep the conflict energies in check. Place a **Rooster with Crown** on your work desk and carry the **Apple Peace Amulet**. Don't let yourself be lured into a fight you cannot win.

Business - *Stay quiet and lie low*

If you are heading a big corporation or running your own, it is better to keep a low profile. Profits may remain low but better that than lose vast chunks of money and even future profits. Hold back on investing or spending on big ticket items. Whatever your decision will come back to haunt you later once the equipment is installed or the investments finalized. Legal woes abound, so if signing legal documents, check all the fine print. Go through all paperwork with a fine tooth comb and a lawyer! Ignorance of the law is no excuse and if sparks fly later, you have no legs to stand on. Check all facts and figures now! You tend to quarrel with all and sundry, from business partners or associates to customers and suppliers, which is no good. Keep all arguments within control so they don't get blown out of proportion. A time to stay quiet and lie low.

Avoid letting off steam on someone you love. If your temper threatens to get out of check, take time out to calm down. Beware saying things you cannot take back.

Love & Relationships - *Maintain the peace*

Maintain peace and harmony by keeping things simple. Don't fight over small things even if you are right. Chances are high you are in the wrong so it makes matter worse! Show extra consideration to your partner since you are the one in a quarrelsome mood. You are more aggressive than usual, shocking your partner and yourself. Calm down and tone down the rhetoric. They have heard it before and you are playing the same old tune.

Home & Family - *Set a good example*

If you have small children, know that your bad mood will rub off on them and affect them adversely which is bad since they are the innocent victims of your impatience. Restrain that anger.

Education - *Watch your manners*

Be considerate since it costs nothing to be polite. If not, you will give important folk a bad impression, and when they think of you next, you will not be their first choice. Ironically, your grades are actually OK and no reason to worry; it is your attitude that is more of the problem! Don't push people away who only have good intentions for you.

11th Month
Dec 7th - Jan 5th 2022

FEELING CONSTANTLY FATIGUED. DON'T WEAR YOURSELF OUT.

Your energy levels take a beating. Whether you are just under the weather or have managed to pile simply way too much on your plate, you will tend to get home each day feeling bushed and battered. Give yourself a break if you need it. Pushing through the fatigue will only lead to careless mistakes. Don't let yourself slide into that downward spiral. The saying "done is better than perfect" does not apply right now. Mistakes made could be costly with long-ranging and multiplier effects. When you feel yourself careering out of control, put on the breaks. Even take a short holiday to clear the mind and refresh. You do no good hoping to go with the flow. Rest! Relax! Then come back to it.

Work & Career - *Feeling fatigued*

Work is a drag as constant fatigue prevents you from doing your job properly though you have the skills. All your projects seem too big for you to handle and completing them on time feels like a heavy weight on your shoulders. You are exhausted physically and mentally, so now is the time to work smart, not hard.

You are in a vulnerable position for others to take advantage of you. Worse, you may be unaware of it happening and unable to stop the exploitation. Do your work in small batches and do not overstretch your capacities. Don't force yourself to work long periods as this will worsen your health and temper. Take short breaks. Go for a walk round the block or even take a nap if possible. Working late nights and heavy socialising are a no-go zone as they will provoke more trouble than pleasure. Devote time for yourself to recharge.

Business - *Double check*

Your health can be a cause for concern so look after it as carefully as your bottom line. Don't work too hard and stress yourself out. Working yourself to the bone is only necessary if your business is collapsing and this is definitely not the case. Important decisions should get a second reading even if they have been scanned before. You might have missed some salient point. Faulty decisions can have bad repercussions that can last for ages. So perhaps letting a professional outsider go through your plans is a good option. Don't try to manage everything yourself. Your analytical capabilities may be clouded with fatigue.

A month when sticking to the status quo is best. Don't change too much.

Love & Relationships - *Secret weapon*

If you are married or in a steady relationship, this augurs a time of joy and satisfaction for all parties. Your partner treats you well and provides the buttress against a tiresome workplace. Knowing you are loved does wonders for your disposition and helps your work life no end. You need all the loving support you can get. Your spouse is your secret weapon. Those single among you could feel the need for a soul mate more acutely now than ever. Don't follow the textbook approach to find a mate. Allow yourself to be unconventional in your tastes for once, and you could surprise and delight yourself with what unfolds

Education - *Feeling under the weather*

Be prepared for all sorts of ailments from catching a cold, getting the sniffles to really falling sick. You may find it harder to concentrate from feeling under the weather. Work at your own pace and don't let yourself get stressed for no reason.

> **CURE FOR THE MONTH:** Carry the **Health Talisman Holder** to strengthen your immunity and to keep the effects of the illness star at bay.

12th Month
Jan 6th - Feb 3rd 2022

PROSPECTS FOR CHANGE LIFTS YOUR SPIRITS

As a new year dawns, things start looking up. It is easy to get excited with new prospects and opportunities that come your way. Others want to work with you and they make the overtures so you don't have to. But you must play your part too! Don't dismiss suggestions to collaborate or these opportunities could slip you by. A month when being pro-active serves you well. Your energy levels return and there is plenty to get your inspired. You are entering a year when your element friend the Tiger takes center stage, and this is no bad thing for you. A time to be bold and to go with your gut feel. Luck is on your side, so be positive and decisive.

Work & Career - *Collaboration*

A busy month with new projects to sink your teeth into and occupy all your waking hours. Lots to keep you busy so you feel productive contributing to the company. You may have to switch department, responsibilities or even job as you have to multi-task incessantly this month. Your superiors think you need to prove your worth, and thus shower you with extra workload. New co-workers enter the scene and while they may seem more qualified, they are not here to make life miserable but to work with you. Do not resent their presence. If anything, learn from them, since they are not here to take or threaten your job. Make every experience part of the learning curve.

Working closely with others benefits you this month. Collaborating with certain individuals could change the course of your whole life.

Business - *Leadership*

You enjoy great leadership luck and those you work with feel motivated by your actions and words. Pay more attention to those under your charge since this is when people from lower ranks can affect you positively. Spend time with subordinates and employees, as they are in a position to point out certain points you may have missed. This is a promising time to initiate new projects and start new systems to increase productivity. While certain steps involve big, physical changes, the blessing is that they can easily be incorporated into existing operations with minimal trauma.

Love & Relationships - *Second chances*

You begin to look at people and events differently and what seemed irrelevant or unacceptable before may appeal for different reasons now! The best advice is to follow your heart. It will not lead you astray or make you fall for someone unsuitable. In fact, it is your head that is causing the trouble, so don't see everything in black and white. Be open and receptive; you may find your soul mate in the most unexpected places or in a person you have previously written off! Never say never. And don't be averse to looking at someone again. Sometimes the second time round is better!

Married Rabbits should however take care to avoid situations that can lead to infidelity and marital woes. The overwhelming presence of love energies could be problematic for the Rabbit who is already happily attached.

Education - *Feeling like a winner*

You are in smooth waters and few things go wrong, so take a deep breath and enjoy! You do well in school and are held up by teachers as a model student. All you need is a little effort and you are on the fast track. While your luck is holding so strong, make the most of it by not resting on your laurels. Work hard, stay motivated, ask questions!

ENHANCER FOR THE MONTH: Boost your stellar luck with the **Windhorse Success Amulet**. Place **Victory Flags** in your home sector of East.